Charcuterie

for
dummies®
A Wiley Brand

Charcuterie

by Mark LaFay

Charcuterie For Dummies®

Published by: **John Wiley & Sons, Inc.,** 111 River Street, Hoboken, NJ 07030-5774, www.wiley.com

Copyright © 2020 by John Wiley & Sons, Inc., Hoboken, New Jersey

Published simultaneously in Canada

For general information on our other products and services, please contact our Customer Care Department within the U.S. at 877-762-2974, outside the U.S. at 317-572-3993, or fax 317-572-4002. For technical support, please visit https://hub.wiley.com/community/support/dummies.

Wiley publishes in a variety of print and electronic formats and by print-on-demand. Some material included with standard print versions of this book may not be included in e-books or in print-on-demand. If this book refers to media such as a CD or DVD that is not included in the version you purchased, you may download this material at http://booksupport.wiley.com. For more information about Wiley products, visit www.wiley.com.

Library of Congress Control Number: 2020904220

ISBN 978-1-119-69078-8 (pbk); ISBN 978-1-119-69079-5 (ebk); ISBN 978-1-119-69074-0 (ebk)

Manufactured in the United States of America

10 9 8 7 6 5 4 3 2 1

Contents at a Glance

Recipes at a Glance

Table of Contents

Introduction

Since as far back as written history takes us, humans have been finding ways to evolve and improve; the result has been a constant evolution in how we live so that life can get easier. Think about the small things, like fire, the wheel, wielding fire, stone tools, metal tools, and so on. Arguably one of the greatest innovations for the human race was learning the art of cultivation and preservation. This led to a shift from a hunter-gatherer way of life to an agrarian culture where animals were domesticated, food was farmed, and methods of preservation were discovered and used so that humankind could weather the storms of four-season living and gradually start spreading out across the world.

Maybe it's this connection to the ways of old that is fueling a resurging interest in seasoning, salting, and preserving meats. Or it could be a pushback against the industrialization of the food system here in the United States. Whether we are romanticizing "the way it used to be" or simply looking for a better way to live in a modern world using influences from the past, the growing interest in artisanal meat craft is apparent.

Charcuterie, a French word, has become a universal term (at least in the U.S.) for preserved meats. However, there is a historical significance to this word. Charcuterie is a craft of maximum utilization and preservation of harvested animals from a time when refrigeration was either limited or nonexistent and animal protein was a luxury, not a staple. Imagine that, a plate filled with potatoes and some meat, not meat and some potatoes. With charcuterie, you can give new life to artifacts of cultural heritage that have, until now, been relegated to the history books.

About This Book

Sometimes the hardest part of trying something new is confronting our fear of the unknown. The goal of this book is to eliminate 90 percent of your fear of working with meat and to give you the tools you need to get started. Crafting delicious fresh and cured meats alike is a pan-cultural skill that has been passed down generationally. The good news is that you don't need to have any prior knowledge about butchery to get started. In fact, you don't even need to have a lot of experience with cooking. This book is designed to give you a breadth of knowledge without too much depth so that it isn't overwhelming.

Part 1 of this book focuses on helping you learn about the gear you will need to get the job done. Let's be honest; the right gear can make a difficult task more manageable. You will learn what gear is used for each task, where to find it, and how to care for it. You will also learn how to stay safe when handling animal proteins. The reason I want to eliminate only 90 percent of your fear is because when working with potentially hazardous food like animal proteins, you need to have a little reverent fear. This will keep you vigilant as you dig in and start processing your meat treats. Finally, you will learn the fundamentals of finding good raw ingredients; the differences among heritage, commodity, and wild proteins; and how to read and navigate recipes.

Part 2 is where you will learn how to make different types of charcuterie. There will be a smattering of whole-muscle, cured meats (think coppa, pancetta, and prosciutto), as well as fresh bacons, sausages, and dry-cured, fermented sausages (salami). You will learn basic methods of processing that will serve as a foundation from which you will be able to build and showcase your creativity. You will also learn how to use modern technology to test your products to ensure safety.

Part 3 of this book will spark your fires of creativity to help you give your best when entertaining with charcuterie. You will learn how to source all sorts of great ingredients to build an epic charcuterie board. You will also get a glimpse at how to incorporate different flavors like sauces, nuts, jams, crackers, breads, and pickled products to build a diverse board where your guests can build all sorts of perfect bites. This section will wrap up with a primer on beer and wine so that you can provide pairings that will take your party to the next level.

And last but not least, the Part of Tens covers ten fantastic wines under $25 to impress your friends when entertaining and ten charcuterie meats you absolutely must try if you get the chance.

Making charcuterie and eating it are equally awesome. *Charcuterie For Dummies* is intended to help you do both.

Foolish Assumptions

We all know what happens when you assume. The goal for *Charcuterie For Dummies* is to make the topic of charcuterie accessible to those who have no prior knowledge of the topic, regardless of whether they are interested in the fabrication of meat or simply entertaining. You heard that right: You do not need any prior knowledge of charcuterie to be able to use this book. In fact, if you have experience in making sausages, bacons, or dry-cured meats, you may find that your experience level exceeds the scope of this book.

Icons Used In This Book

As you read this book, you'll see icons in the margins that indicate material of interest (or not, as the case may be). This section briefly describes each of these icons.

TIP

Tips are nice because they help you save time or perform some task without a lot of extra work. The tips in this book are timesaving techniques, or pointers to resources that you should check out.

WARNING

At the risk of sounding like an alarmist, anything marked with a warning is something you should pay close attention to. Proceed with caution if you must proceed at all.

REMEMBER

If you don't get anything else out of a particular chapter or section, remember the material marked by this icon. This text will remind you of meaningful content that you should file away. It might also remind you of something that was already covered and that is useful again.

Beyond the Book

This book also comes with a free online Cheat Sheet full of tips related to making and entertaining with charcuterie. Go to www.dummies.com and search for "Charcuterie For Dummies Cheat Sheet."

Where To Go From Here

Its go-time! The world of charcuterie is at your fingertips; you just have to turn the page and get started. Pick a pace you're comfortable with and just dive in. The first chapter is dedicated to gear. If you already have the gear, or don't need help finding, using, or caring for it, then skip to the next chapter. Make sure you don't skip over the chapter on sanitation and safe handling, though. Give it at least one pass and then reference it whenever you have doubts. Other than that, pop around and have fun.

I laid out the book so that you can start anywhere and not necessarily have to read it in a linear fashion. Regardless of how you tackle the topic, *Charcuterie For Dummies* will get you going on your way toward meaty mastery.

1

Getting Started With Charcuterie

Chapter **1**

Get the Gear

In any craft, an artisan has a specific set of tools to help get the job done. Having the right tools for the job makes it much easier to execute successfully. For example, you can use any number of blunt objects to knock a nail into a board, but the right tool for that job is a hammer. Hammers make nailing much easier. Taking it step further, a nail gun would make nailing even easier than using a hammer. Regardless of how big, bad, and awesome your tools are, the correct tool is essential for doing a job well.

Successfully making sausages, bacon, cured meats, or any other type of charcuterie, requires very specific tools and equipment. Using the right equipment not only simplifies the process of crafting meats, but also helps you make products that are safe to eat. In this chapter, I identify the various tools that you need to execute the processes in this book. Of course, the right tool is just the starting point; you also need to know how to use that tool. Proper use of your tools is critical to achieving great results. In this chapter, you learn how to find the right tools, use those tools, care for them, and stay safe with them.

Meat Grinders

Meat grinders are specialized machines designed for the sole purpose of breaking pieces of meat and fat into smaller pieces by forcing them through a metal plate containing several small holes. Not all meat grinders are equal, and several factors differentiate them, including the following:

>> Power source (electric or manual)

>> Speed of grinding

>> Volume of grinding

>> Size of the grinder

>> Construction of the grinder

All grinders can be broken down into the same core parts, and understanding what each part does will help you decide which grinder is right for you. These parts are shown in Figure 1-1 and include the following:

>> **Body and hopper.** The body and hopper is generally one solid piece and houses all of the moving parts (excluding the motor).

>> **Worm (auger).** The worm is inserted into the motor through the body. This is the screw-like part that draws meat down the hopper and through the body toward the knife.

>> **Knife.** The knife is a cutting implement with four blades and looks like a propeller on a plane. The knife fits onto the end of the worm and spins at the same rate. As the meat passes down the body via the worm, it is first cut by the knife as it is forced through the plate.

>> **Plate.** The plate is a thick, round piece of steel containing several holes. It fits onto the end of the body and holds the worm in position as it spins. The size of the holes on the plate determines how coarse or fine your ground meat will be.

>> **Locking ring.** The locking ring holds the plate in place, securing all of the moving parts of your grinder.

For the purposes of this book, I will discuss three types of meat grinders. The size of the grinder you choose will be largely determined by the amount of meat that you plan to grind. This will also determine the size of the grinder you choose.

FIGURE 1-1:
Meat grinder
parts.

Photo by David Pluimer

Manual meat grinders

Manual meat grinders are exactly what you might imagine: grinders that are human powered. The working parts are the same as previously described, but instead of an electric motor to turn the worm and knife, you have a hand crank, as shown in Figure 1-2.

Manual meat grinders cost less than electric meat grinders because they don't contain any motorized parts. This is probably how your grandma or grandpa used to make sausage. Manual meat grinders must be clamped onto a hard surface like a table- or countertop. Manual meat grinders are lower in cost and maintenance than their electric workhorse big brothers, which is why they are a great starting point. Manual grinders can also be used anywhere because they do not require electricity.

KitchenAid mixer attachment grinder

Several years ago I bought my wife a KitchenAid mixer for Christmas. In all honesty, I bought it for myself but told my wife it was for her. This was a wonderful upgrade to our kitchen because of all the delightful baked goods we could make without all the excessive manual labor. I'm kind of like Tim "The Tool Man" Taylor: I like more power when it comes to my cooking tools!

FIGURE 1-2:
Manual meat
grinder.

If you happen to have a KitchenAid mixer, then you'll notice that the front of the mixer has a place for attaching add-on equipment. One of the attachments you can purchase from KitchenAid for your mixer is a meat grinder, pictured in Figure 1-3.

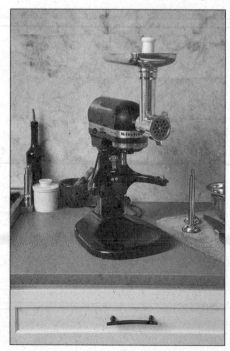

FIGURE 1-3:
KitchenAid
attachment port
and grinder
attachment.

Photo by David Pluimer

The KitchenAid grinder attachment is great for testing the waters of making sausage. The parts are all the same as on a manual grinder, but you get a nice upgrade from the laborious task of manually grinding by using the grinder attachment with your KitchenAid mixer. This is, however, not a good long-term solution. Your mixer was specifically designed as a mixer, not a meat grinder, and so excessive use as a grinder with the attachment can greatly shorten the lifespan of your KitchenAid mixer.

Electric meat grinders

As you navigate your own internal decision tree, give yourself a little time when it comes to selecting your meat grinder. Unless you have compelling reasons for not getting an electric grinder, like budget or access to power, this is where you should really focus your research. Electric meat grinders are the right tool for the job when it comes to grinding meat! They come in all shapes and sizes, which are largely determined by the intended volume of use. As with the KitchenAid attachment and the manual meat grinder, the parts of an electric meat grinder are the same with the exception of the electric motor, as shown in Figure 1-4.

FIGURE 1-4:
Electric meat
grinder.

Photo by David Pluimer

Budget and intended use are major determining factors when selecting a meat grinder. If you plan to use your meat grinder more than once a year or to grind more than ten pounds of meat at a time, then you should consider an electric grinder. This will save you time, energy, and blisters.

Sizing and choosing your grinder

Grinder size is determined by the size of the plate that the grinder uses.

REMEMBER

The plate is a circular piece of steel covered in holes that fits on the end of the worm and determines how coarse or fine your ground meat will be.

The grinder size is denoted by a number, and this number corresponds to the diameter of the plate. The correlation of grinder size to plate size is shown in the following table:

Grinder Size	5	8	12	22	32
Diameter of Plate	2 1/8"	2 1/2"	2 3/4"	3 1/4"	3 7/8"

Generally speaking, the larger the size of the grinder, the larger the motor, and thus the higher the cost of the grinder. If you are planning to use your grinder a few times a year to grind less than a few hundred pounds of meat, then you can definitely get by with a number 5 or 8 grinder. For a comparison, Figure 1-5 illustrates some of the different sizes of grinder plates up to number 32.

FIGURE 1-5:
Sausage grinder plates of different sizes.

Photo by David Pluimer

One other determining factor when choosing a grinder is the materials from which your grinder is made. Stainless steel is the industry standard because it is durable, easy to clean, and resistant to rust. However, you can save money by going with plastic or aluminum options.

Sausage Stuffers

A sausage stuffer's job is simple: to get ground meat into some sort of casing. There are a few types of sausage stuffer, but the most useful stuffer is called a *vertical sausage stuffer* (see Figure 1-6). Strictly speaking, stuffers are quite simple and are composed of the following parts:

>> **Cylinder.** The cylinder holds your meat mixture.

>> **Piston.** The piston fits perfectly into the cylinder and forces your meat mixture down through the cylinder. The piston is forced down by a hand crank.

>> **Horn.** The horn attaches to the bottom of the cylinder and is the approximate diameter of the sausage you are stuffing. Your casing fits onto the horn.

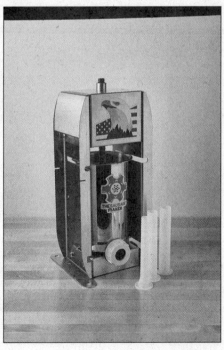

FIGURE 1-6:
Vertical stuffer
and parts.

Photo by David Pluimer

Vertical stuffers are ideal because their orientation gives you the greatest mechanical advantage as you crank the piston down. They are also ideal for stuffing a wet mixture like the emulsified sausages discussed in Chapter 6.

Cranking a stuffer can at times require some shoulder and arm strength. Depending on how firm your meat mixture is, you will want to make sure that the stuffer you select either comes with clamps to hold it down to your work surface, or at minimum has enough surface area on the base of the stuffer to use bench clamps like the ones pictured in Figure 1-7.

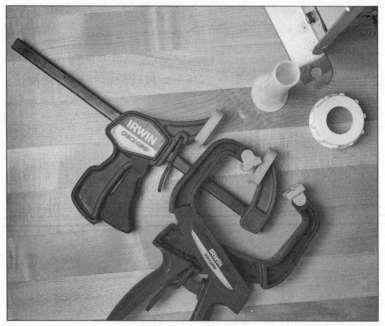

FIGURE 1-7:
Bench clamps for your stuffer.

Photo by David Pluimer

Meat Slicer

The meat slicer (a.k.a. deli slicer) is a motorized device for easily and uniformly slicing meats. Meat slicers come in all shapes and sizes (like the one shown in Figure 1-8), and while they are not absolutely mission-critical for making meats, they are extremely helpful when you get to finishing up your bacon, or other meats from which you want to have slices ready to go.

Photo by David Pluimer

A seemingly endless number of meat slicers are available. The usefulness of your slicer will be largely determined by the size of the product that you plan to slice. If the sole purpose of your deli slicer will be to slice bacon, then you will want, at minimum, a 10-inch slicer — and possibly a 12-inch slicer — depending on the size of the pork belly you want to slice. Popular and reliable brands of slicers include

>> Berkel

>> Bizerba

>> Hobart

>> Globe

Several consumer brands with lower-end and lower-cost options are also available.

Smokers

A great smokehouse is a great thing! Have you ever had barbeque that made you groan with contentment? Or, how about bacon that kept you coming back for another strip? Have you ever wept when the last piece of bacon was eaten? Asking for a friend.

There are several ways to smoke, and there are several outcomes that you can have. The most important quality in a smoker is whether or not you can run it and make tasty food that is safe to eat. For the purposes of this book, I focus on hot smoking, which is smoking at temperatures over 100 degrees Fahrenheit. The goal is to cook your product to a temperature that kills off any potentially harmful bacteria, while applying a smoke flavor to the meat. Following is a list of smokers you can buy.

» **Electric smoker:** Electric smokers (see Figure 1-9) are a delightful creation because they offer automated digital temperature control. Electric smokers also smolder wood chips using an electric heating element which requires no lighting or maintaining. You can acquire an electric smoker for your home at a reasonable price, and aside from the periodic requirement to reload it with wood chips, it will be largely "set and forget."

FIGURE 1-9:
Electric smoker.

The Sausage Maker

» **Pellet smoker:** Pellet smokers are fully automated electric smokers. These smokers use compressed hardwood sawdust that is held together with paraffin to generate heat and smoke. Did I mention that they are fully automated? The smoke is never as heavy as you'll get with an electric wood chip smoker, but you do get a whole lot of convenience.

» **Gas-burning smoker:** Gas-burning smokers (see Figure 1-10) are more like a traditional grill in that they use a propane burner to generate heat and smolder the wood in order to generate smoke. Gas burners require frequent monitoring to ensure that you are getting a steady heat output. The benefit is that you can smolder larger pieces of wood, which some enthusiasts would argue gives you a better smoke flavor.

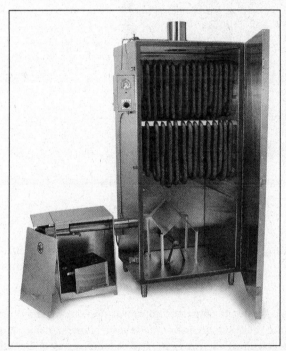

FIGURE 1-10:
Gas-burning
smoker.

The Sausage Maker

Curing Chambers

Later in this book, you learn how to make dry-cured meats like salami and prosciutto. In order to dry-cure meat, you need to be able to control temperature, humidity, and airflow. Unless you have a sweet 200-year-old barn in the hills of Tuscany, it can be a chore to replicate the type of environment you will need to produce dry-cured products. Never fear, though; you have a couple of options. Your first option is to purchase a dry-curing chamber like the one pictured in Figure 1-11.

FIGURE 1-11: Ready made dry-curing chamber.

The Sausage Maker

The dry-curing chamber controls both its internal humidity and temperature to ensure you get slow, controlled drying. The downside to this type of device is the cost.

Your second option is to construct your own dry-curing chamber. You can do this with a working refrigerator, and some relatively inexpensive sensors and controls like those pictured in Figure 1-12. The detailed process for building your own chamber is outside the scope of this book. However, if there's an internet search engine, there's a way!

FIGURE 1-12:
Humidity and temperature control sensors for a homemade curing chamber.

Auber Instruments

Scientific Meters

Humans have been preserving meats without modern technology for a few thousand years now. Methods of fermenting (to control acidity of meat), salting, and drying have been handled by family lore, which often included tracking.

Today we have the benefit of a great deal of science that has helped shed light on why things were done a certain way. *Shelf stability* is a term used to describe the condition of a food product that doesn't need refrigeration. You create shelf stability in meat by controlling the amount of water (water activity, a_w) in the meat through salting and drying. In the case of salami, you also manage it by increasing the acidity of the meat, which is measured in pH.

Water activity meter

Explaining water activity in a straightforward manner is no simple task. It is a scientific way of determining how much water is available in something. Water is required for bacteria and other organic pathogens to be able to live and replicate. As a result, the best way to limit the growth of bacteria, which can be potentially harmful and cause spoilage, is to eliminate as much of the water as possible. A substantial amount of research is available on the internet to explain the correlation between water activity and shelf stability.

Water activity (a_w) meters are largely cost prohibitive for the home enthusiast, so I will focus on Old World methods of tracking water loss through weight loss over time to determine the safety of your meat products. However, if you have the resources and the desire to take that extra step toward safety, the leading producer of water activity meters is the METER Group.

pH meter

With food, acidity is best described as how sour something tastes; the more sour it is, the more acidic it is. When making salami, one of the requirements for safety is to lower the pH — that is, to make it acidic — so that bacteria is unable to grow in the interior of the salami while it dries. There are many ways to increase acidity (lower pH), which you will learn about in Chapter 7. You will find that pH meters are both affordable and necessary when you start making your own salami. There is no way to safely approximate the pH of a meat product without testing it.

Small Wares

In addition to the larger specialized tools and equipment that you will need to successfully craft your meats, you will also need a handful of other smaller tools.

>> **Knives:** Knives are highly personal. There is not one size that fits all when choosing knives; however, a flexible or semi-flexible boning knife and a hard chef's knife will serve you well.

>> **Cutting boards:** You can never have enough cutting boards. You should only use plastic cutting boards, because they can be cleaned and sanitized with ease. Wood looks cool, but unless it is a properly sealed hardwood cutting board, it can lead to trouble.

>> **Sausage pricker:** These are small tools intended for pricking sausages to let air bubbles out.

>> **Scales:** Scales that measure in grams and ounces are ideal for accurately measuring salts, nitrates, spices, and so on. Larger scales for weighing larger quantities of meat are also a necessity.

>> **Metal bowls and tubs:** Large mixing bowls or plastic tubs are a must for holding both ground and unground meats.

Properly Caring for Your Gear

Once you've made an investment in equipment, you will want to take good care of it so that it lasts a long time, and also to keep you and the beneficiaries of your hobby safe and healthy! All of your equipment must be properly cleaned with warm, soapy water and then disinfected with some sort of sanitizer like a bleach-and-water mixture.

TIP

You can disinfect with a solution of one tablespoon of bleach to one gallon of cold water. If the water is hot, then the chlorine will evaporate off, so be sure to use cold water. Immerse the equipment in the mixture and then let it air dry.

Once you've cleaned and disinfected your equipment, if there are any rubber gaskets or stainless steel parts that require some sort of lubrication, be sure to apply it per the manufacturer's specifications.

REMEMBER

Only store your gear after it has dried completely.

Caring for your grinder

Properly cleaning a meat grinder requires a little TLC. Meats and spices tend to clump inside the hopper, as well as in the threads of the locking ring. You may need a small wire brush to break these particles free. This can be particularly arduous if you have any sugar in your recipe, as it can quickly become sticky. A high-pressure spray setting on your sink faucet can also assist in pushing particles through the small holes of the grinder plate. Be sure to thoroughly inspect the grinder before sanitizing it and leaving it to dry.

Once your grinder parts are dry, you can avoid rust by applying food-safe mineral oil all over the parts that experience the greatest amount of friction. If you find a little bit of rust, don't fret. Use lemon juice and a rag to remove the rust, then properly lubricate the parts with food-safe mineral oil.

Caring for your stuffer

Much like a meat grinder, a sausage stuffer isn't the easiest thing in the world to clean. You'll want to be sure to inspect the cylinder, piston, and horns for pesky particulate that may be hiding. They tend to stick to welded seams, and in the threads where the locking rings screw on. The inside of your stuffing horns can also be a place where meat hides out. Investing in some tube brushes like the ones pictured in Figure 1-13 will serve you well.

FIGURE 1-13:
Tube brushes for
cleaning stuffing
horns.

Photo by David Pluimer

The piston of your stuffer will have a rubber gasket around the outside. Remove the gasket, and clean it and the piston with soapy water before sanitizing it. You also want to remove the pressure release valve on your piston and clean the valve and the hole where it is fitted. Once the stuffer is cleaned and sanitized, make sure to lubricate the piston gasket with food-safe mineral oil. This will keep the rubber from drying out prematurely.

Shopping for Gear Locally

If you live in a larger municipality where you have access to more retail options, then shopping for your gear locally may be the way to go. A good place to start is by checking in with your local family butcher to see where they prefer to shop. You may find that there are great butcher supply stores under your nose that you never knew about!

If you don't have a specialized butcher supply store, then you'll want to look for a restaurant supplier. Here in Indianapolis, a great option is Central Restaurant Products. This is a local company that has been in the area for decades. The biggest benefits to shopping local are that you keep your dollars in your local economy and, above all else, that you can talk to the suppliers in person. There is something special about having a go-to person to help you eliminate guesswork.

Shopping for Gear Online

If you don't have the luxury of shopping for equipment locally, then you can still get that in-store feel by shopping online; however, you have to know what you are looking for! A quick Google search for meat grinders or sausage stuffers will bring you a litany of options and may actually seem overwhelming. Buying new equipment with which you have very little experience can be daunting. It can be hard to know how to balance the desire for a low price with the need for high quality. The old adage, "You get what you pay for," really applies when shopping for meat processing equipment. You can buy almost anything on Amazon.com, but the problem with large sites like Amazon is that it can be hard to sift through the junk.

Keep in mind that when shopping for your equipment, especially the higher-dollar items, you want to buy from an online retailer who will stand by their products and provide quality customer service. Following are some sites that I often frequent.

>> **Sausagemaker.com:** This is a family-run business located in Buffalo, New York. They have everything you need to get the job done and then some on top of that! The Sausage Maker provides some of the best customer service in the business. If you get a faulty product, or something doesn't hold up as advertised, then they will solve the problem and take care of you. Figure 1-14 shows the homepage of their website.

>> **Butcher-packer.com:** Located in Madison Heights, Michigan, Butcher and Packer has all the equipment you could need. Their costs are also in line with those of their competitors, and they stand by their products. However, they don't have quite the product options of sausagemaker.com.

>> **Waltonsinc.com:** Walton's is another Midwestern family-owned business. They have a large selection of products, and they provide great customer service.

FIGURE 1-14:
Sausagemaker.
com homepage.

Source: Sausagemaker.com

IN THIS CHAPTER

» **Learning basic sanitation**

» **Understanding pathogens of concern**

» **Navigating safe handling of animal proteins**

» **Relying on science**

Chapter **2**

Working with Potentially Hazardous Food

There is nothing worse than sitting down to dinner where someone at the table starts a conversation about something, dare I say, gross. You know what kind of topics I'm talking about: things that would be considered uncouth. For the sake of manners, make sure you aren't sitting at the dinner table when you dig into the next few pages. When it comes to food handling, safety must be of paramount importance to you. In fact, you can't be a good food artisan if you can't manage basic hygiene and sanitation. It is so easy to make yourself sick if you don't take every possible precaution when handling food.

I'll take it a step further, though. When it comes to working with potentially hazardous food, like meat, there are additional safeguards that must be in place to ensure your safety as well as the safety of anyone who may ingest your creations. Think I'm joking? According to the Centers for Disease Control and Prevention (CDC), in 2016 there were an estimated 36 million cases of foodborne illness in America. That means that approximately one in every ten people got sick once that year from food. About 30 million of those cases could have been avoided simply through adherence to a proper personal hygiene program in and outside of the kitchen (`https://www.cdc.gov/foodborneburden/pdfs/scallan-estimated-illnesses-foodborne-pathogens.pdf`).

I won't bore you with the details here (that's for later); in this chapter you will learn basic sanitation, hygiene, and safe food handling skills. You will also learn about pathogens of concern and how to safeguard against them with strategies backed by science.

Personal Hygiene

As a kid, I used to get so irritated when my parents would harp on me to wash behind my ears and in my belly button (God must have used a melon baller when he made my belly button). But this isn't the type of personal hygiene that is of concern here. Well, it is and it isn't. Before you can even think about working with food meant for human consumption, you need to be thinking about cleanliness and sanitation, and that starts with you. Hand washing is the first thing that you should do. According to the Food and Drug Administration (FDA), you should wash your hands with warm water and lather up with antibacterial soap for at least 12 seconds before rinsing and drying your hands with a single-use towel. So count them off: one-Mississippi, two-Mississippi, you get the point! Once you've washed your hands, consider yourself scrubbed in for surgery.

Here is a list of activities that will (should) trigger a rewash:

>> Touching your phone

>> Touching your face

>> Touching your hair

>> Touching money

>> Putting your hands in your pockets

>> Touching a door handle

>> Touching trash

>> Eating food

>> Sneezing or coughing into your hands

>> Before or when changing gloves

I could go on, but I'm sure you get the point. Keep your hands clean.

Aprons

Wearing an apron isn't nearly as obvious as ritual handwashing may be, but it is definitely important. The clothes you are wearing are likely to have come into contact with all sorts of potential contagions throughout the day. If the food you are working with happens to come into contact with your clothing, then you can consider it contaminated. An easy way to deal with this is by wearing an apron like the one pictured in Figure 2-1.

Photo by David Pluimer

FIGURE 2-1:
A standard kitchen apron.

Before putting on your apron, make sure it is clean and hasn't been used prior to you putting it on. Not only will the apron keep you clean when working with food, but it will also protect your food against unintended contamination.

Hair restraints

You know this has happened to you before. You went out to lunch, and took a bite of your mac and cheese only to be startled by a sudden flossing sensation. Hair in food isn't sanitary and it isn't appetizing. A proper hair restraint will save you and your family from the unintended gross-out of finding a hair in your sausage. A simple hair net, baseball cap, or sock hat will work. If you have long hair, pulling it back and putting it up will be critical as well.

Food-safe gloves

Since working in food service, I've grown accustomed to using food-safe gloves for almost everything I do with food, regardless of whether it's at work or at home. Food-safe gloves are an extra barrier of protection. They aren't as necessary when handling food that must be cooked before it can be eaten. They are, however, an absolute necessity if you are handling food that is ready to eat, like salamis and whole-muscle charcuterie, which I discuss later in this book. Figure 2-2 shows some food-safe gloves.

FIGURE 2-2:
Stay safe with food-safe gloves.

Photo by David Pluimer

Gloves meant for food handling can be plastic or latex, and they can be powder lined or powder free. The powder makes it easier to slip the gloves on if your hands are still slightly damp from you washing them before putting them on.

Before You Get Started

Before you start handling food, you need to make sure that your work area and tools are all cleaned and sanitized. In a commercial setting, this is called a *pre-op*, which is short for pre-operational. At this point you will need to fill a small bowl or bucket with soapy water and another bucket with sanitizer, which can be a blend of bleach and water. You also need a separate clean towel to use with each bucket.

You can disinfect with a solution of one tablespoon of bleach to one gallon of cold water. If it's hot, the chlorine will evaporate off, so be sure to use cold water.

Once your cleaner and sanitizer buckets are ready to go, clean down each work surface with the soapy water and then wipe it down with the sanitizer.

Once you have cleaned and sanitized each surface, clean and sanitize all of the tools and equipment you intend to use. These include knives, cutting boards, bowls, and any other object or device that will come in contact with food. Last but not least, you will want to visually inspect any device you will be using, like your grinder or stuffer, to make sure there aren't any food particles that you missed the last time it was cleaned and put away.

One way to avoid missing any of these details is to put together a prep list, like the one shown in Figure 2-3. You can print this list and have it in the kitchen for when you get started, and then simply check off the items as you clean and sanitize them.

Once you've checked everything off your list, you're ready to get started.

Cleaning Prep-List

Description	Cleaned	Sanitized
Counter Top		
Refrigerator Handle		
Sausage Grinder & Parts		
Sausage Stuffer & Parts		
Cutting Boards		
Knives		
Utensils		

FIGURE 2-3:
'Clean and Sanitize' prep list.

Mark LaFay

TIP

You should also create a checklist that you can use when you're finished in the kitchen. This is a good way to make sure everything is properly cleaned and sanitized before you put it away.

Protecting Against Pathogens of Concern

Proper procedures for hygiene and workspace sanitation, if done correctly, will prevent you from contaminating the meats that you are working with. However, you also need to be aware of pathogens that are commonly found in the different animal species that you may be working with. Over the last several decades, the U.S. Department of Agriculture (USDA) and the Food Safety and Inspection Service (FSIS) have done a lot of work with farmers, food processors, food scientists, and research organizations like universities, to improve and enhance food safety guidelines to help reduce foodborne illnesses. That said, food safety ultimately requires proper handling of food once you bring it home.

Common interventions to control or kill bacteria

Numerous types of bacteria are found in all living creatures, and can cause food spoilage or even severe illness. The chances of you coming into contact with these naughty bacteria will be much lower if you have a basic understanding of how to control the growth of bacteria and how to properly kill them through interventions while you're processing meat. Common interventions include

>> Salting

>> Adding nitrites and nitrates

>> Acidifying to lower pH

>> Drying to lower water activity (a_w)

Raw sausages that require a cooking step before consumption require very little intervention because heat treating by cooking, when done correctly, will kill all bacteria.

The FSIS has published a document known as *Appendix A — Compliance Guidelines For Meeting Lethality Performance Standards For Certain Meat And Poultry Products*. This document contains guidelines that are used by most, if not all, food processors in America. The table from the appendix is shown in Figure 2-4 and lists the temperature, and associated amount of time that a product must be held at that temperature, required to be lethal to all bacteria.

Minimum Internal Temperature		Minimum processing time in minutes or seconds after minimum temperature is reached	
Degrees Fahrenheit	Degrees Centigrade	6.5-$\log_{10}$ Lethality	7-$\log_{10}$ Lethality
130	54.4	112 min.	121 min.
131	55.0	89 min.	97 min.
132	55.6	71 min.	77 min.
133	56.1	56 min.	62 min.
134	56.7	45 min.	47 min.
135	57.2	36 min.	37 min.
136	57.8	28 min.	32 min.
137	58.4	23 min.	24 min.
138	58.9	18 min.	19 min.
139	59.5	15 min.	15 min.
140	60.0	12 min.	12 min.
141	60.6	9 min.	10 min.
142	61.1	8 min.	8 min.
143	61.7	6 min.	6 min.
144	62.2	5 min.	5 min.
145	62.8	4 min.*	4 min.*
146	63.3	169 sec.	182 sec.
147	63.9	134 sec.	144 sec.
148	64.4	107 sec.	115 sec.
149	65.0	85 sec.	91 sec.
150	65.6	67 sec.	72 sec.
151	66.1	54 sec.	58 sec.
152	66.7	43 sec.	46 sec.
153	67.2	34 sec.	37 sec.
154	67.8	27 sec.	29 sec.
155	68.3	22 sec.	23 sec.
156	68.9	17 sec.	19 sec.
157	69.4	14 sec.	15 sec.
158	70.0	0 sec.**	0 sec.**
159	70.6	0 sec.**	0 sec.**
160	71.1	0 sec **	0 sec.**

* Past regulations have listed the minimum processing time for roast beef cooked to 145°F as "Instantly." However, due to their large size, most of these roasts dwell at 145°F, or even at higher temperatures, for at least 4 minutes after the minimum internal temperature is reached. FSIS has revised this time/temperature table to reflect this and emphasizes that, to better ensure compliance with the performance standard, establishments should ensure a dwell time of at least 4 minutes if 145°F is the minimum internal temperature employed.

** The required lethalities are achieved instantly when the internal temperature of a cooked meat product reaches 158°F or above.

Source: FSIS

FIGURE 2-4: Time and temperature table from FSIS *Appendix A.*

Temperature control

An important factor in controlling the growth of bacteria is proper temperature control. Did your parents ever yell at you to shut the fridge door? My folks did. Probably more so because it caused the fridge to run and use up electricity. But the reality is that spoilage of food happens more quickly at warmer temperatures. That's because bacteria like to grow when the conditions are warmer.

When processing meat, you want to keep your proteins as cold as possible throughout the process. This will result in a higher-quality product, as well as a safer product. When you are storing meat for processing, you want to store it as close to the freezing point as possible without freezing it. When processing, you want to keep your meat mixtures cold, but this can be difficult when cutting, grinding, stuffing, and so on because of the time the meat is out of refrigeration, coupled with the added friction that comes with grinding and stuffing.

Several years ago, Dr. Bruce Tompkin presented the results of a study, titled "The significance of time-temperature to growth of foodborne pathogens during refrigeration at 40–50°F." These results showed that you can safely process pork, chicken, and beef at temperatures above 60 degrees Fahrenheit and still be safe. However, it isn't ideal for producing a quality product. So, to be safe and to ensure the best results, you should use a digital temperature probe such as the one shown in Figure 2-5.

FIGURE 2-5:
Temperature
probe.

Photo by David Pluimer

TIP

When you start handling meat, take the temperature of the meat and jot it down. When you are done working with the meat, record the temperature and the time again. Be sure to keep the temperature below 45 degrees Fahrenheit at all times.

Pathogens of Concern

Food poisoning is nasty and can be scary. The best way to have confidence in the work you are doing is to know the risks, call them by name, and understand the best way to manage the risks. There are a handful of bacteria that can be present in different types of proteins, and there are a handful of ways to mitigate the risk of these bacteria. In the case of raw sausages that require a cook step prior to consumption, cooking will be your final line of defense. A good understanding of each pathogen of concern and its respective Achilles heal will help build confidence in your processes and ultimately help you stay safe!

Salmonella

Salmonella is probably the most commonly known bacteria simply because of its prevalence in undercooked chicken. This is why even to this day, a well-cooked piece of chicken is heated to 160 degrees Fahrenheit. This can give it the consistency of rubber if done too well, but, hey, better safe than sorry. *Salmonella* is a concern in poultry and to a lesser extent in pork. *Salmonella* can be controlled by lowering the meat's pH (acidifying). Cooking to 160 degrees Fahrenheit will also kill it.

Staphylococcus

Staphylococcus, or Staph, may exist on the surface of some meat and poultry, but it is largely introduced into food through human contact. It can be controlled through acidification. A cooking step will also kill it. Your best tools in combatting it are proper hygiene, and cleaning and sanitation of your work area before, during, and after food contact.

Campylobacter

Campylobacter is found in both poultry and pork, though less commonly in the latter. It is controlled by temperature, drying, and acidification.

Listeria monocytogenes

Listeria monocytogenes is commonly found in ready-to-eat food products. It can make healthy people feel like they have the flu, but it can also cause meningitis or even be terminal in elderly people, infants, and pregnant women. This particular bacteria is pretty tough to beat. Your best bet at home is to be thorough with your sanitation.

Clostridium botulinum and *C. perfringens*

I learned about botulism at a very young age, grocery shopping with my father. It almost became a game where I would look for the cans that had swollen tops. Those were the ones that you knew were bad. I would then turn them in to the customer service desk and feel like a super hero. Botulism is a pretty serious disease caused by the *C. botulinum* toxin. This toxin thrives in low- to no-oxygen environments (think vacuum bags, smokers, and the inside of a sausage). You can control it with sodium nitrite and acidification (by lowering the pH).

Escherichi coli O157:H7

There are numerous types of *Escherichi coli* (*E. coli*) in the world. The big, bad one that causes recalls of food 100 percent of the time is a specific strain of *E. coli* referred to as O157:H7. This is the stuff that will cause serious illness and potentially death if not treated immediately. *E. coli* is generally an issue only for beef. Cows, when processed under USDA inspection, undergo prevention measures for O157 to ensure it is not spread if it is present. That said, if you decide to work with beef to make a sausage or an air-dried beef product like bresaola, you may want to take a preventative measure of your own to further ensure you don't spread it.

TIP

One common way to further ensure that your beef is O157 free is to spray it down with a three-percent vinegar solution. To make three-percent vinegar solution, follow these steps:

1. **Pour 6 ounces of distilled vinegar of 5 percent strength into a spray bottle.**

2. **Pour 4 ounces of distilled water into the spray bottle.**

3. **Shake to mix.**

Lightly mist your beef with the spray and let it rest in the fridge overnight before you continue.

Trichinella

This isn't a bacteria but it's gross nonetheless. Trichinella is a small roundworm that is fairly common. Many controls have been put in place on the farming and processing side to reduce the presence of Trichinella in pork, almost to the point of eradication. However, it is still worth getting familiar with this problem, especially if you work with wild game. Trichinella can be controlled by deep freezing your protein first, which requires a long period of time at a deep-freeze temperature. You can also control it by drying.

There is a lot of information to be found through online research on how to manage and control the spread of Trichinosis. The USDA provides some very helpful guidelines that can be viewed online here:

https://www.fsis.usda.gov/wps/wcm/connect/2ca75475-3efd-4fa7-8f34-7393c245a1df/Trichinella-Compliance-Guide-03162016.pdf?MOD=AJPERES

How to Find Help

The first time that you make charcuterie, you may find yourself doubting your abilities. This is a very normal occurrence the first few times you craft something on your own. It may even be the case the 100th time you make something. The more you hone your skills, the more variables you will encounter and the more you will learn what is within the realm of safe or "normal." But until you become more comfortable, there will be those moments where you will want reassurance beyond the food "smelling okay."

If you live in a town where there is a commercial producer of charcuterie, you can always reach out to them to see if they can provide some professional guidance. But in most cases, your best bet will be to turn to online resources. Following are a few great options. (Note: You will need a Facebook profile in order to join these communities.) Figure 2-6 is a picture of the Salt Cured Pig Facebook group where thousands of enthusiasts and professionals share recipes and procedures for their creations.

- » The Salt Cured Pig (https://www.facebook.com/groups/thesaltcuredpig/)
- » Sausage Debauchery (https://www.facebook.com/groups/sausagedebauchery/)
- » Cured Meats and Sausage Making (https://www.facebook.com/groups/CuredMeats/)

FIGURE 2-6:
The Salt Cured
Pig Facebook
page.

REMEMBER

When joining an online community like those listed here, there is a universal code of ethics that you should follow to avoid frustrating other users or, at worst, getting kicked out. These online communities have been developed to help members learn and teach about crafting meats. The following is a list of guidelines you will want to strictly adhere to:

>> **Read first.** Before you start asking questions, be proactive in the search for your answers. Scroll through the groups to see what other users are posting and how the conversations have gone. This is a great way to discover ideas for new things to try. You may also find that other people have had the same struggles that you have.

>> **Search is your friend.** Facebook provides search features (Figure 2-7) that will simplify your search within a group. Save yourself time and headaches by searching the group for the content you need before asking.

>> **Provide recipes and procedures.** If you can't find the answers you are looking for, post your question in the group. However, you will need to arm the group with as much information as possible so that they can provide real assistance. You will need to post good-quality pictures of the item with which you are having difficulty. You will also need to provide the recipe and describe your process.

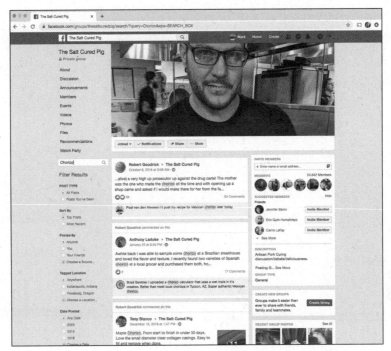

FIGURE 2-7:
Facebook search
feature.

Source: Facebook

WARNING

If, after you've consulted all available resources, you still feel uncomfortable with a product you've crafted, pitch it. There is no sense in taking a risk at making yourself, or someone else, sick. Go with your gut. You're better off throwing something away, and having nothing to show for your time, efforts, and money, than making yourself sick.

Chapter **3**

Quality In, Quality Out

A t some point or another, you probably remember someone telling you that "you are what you eat." For the most part, this is an accurate statement. The food we eat is converted into tissue mass, bone density, and muscular strength, and it keeps the proverbial fire of our metabolism burning. There is a direct correlation between the quality of food we ingest and our body's ability to perform the jobs for which it was designed. It is safe to say that garbage in equals garbage out, or that quality in equals quality out. I'm oversimplifying here, but the reality is the same for the food you create.

The quality of the ingredients that you start with will largely impact the quality of the end product. Don't get me wrong; all sorts of wizardry can occur in the kitchen to make something amazing out of something subpar. Think back to some of your most memorable meals. They were likely made with very simple yet high-quality ingredients that were prepared well to create a delicious meal. This applies to everything you do with charcuterie; the quality of your raw materials will greatly affect the quality of your end product.

The way an animal is bred, how it is raised, what it is fed, where it is fed, and how it is dispatched (fancy word for slaughtered) all play a role in the quality of the protein from that animal. The same goes for all dry and fresh ingredients added during processing. In this chapter you will learn about commodity protein versus heritage protein, and the benefits of pasture-raised proteins. You will also learn how to set yourself up for success with wild game. Last but not least, you will learn the value of salts and spices and how they serve as the missing link between food for now and food for later.

Thinking Twice about Commodity Protein

The next time you walk through a grocery store, take a stroll through the meat department and look at all of the nice, neat little packages of cut meat. Steaks, chops, and chicken breasts all rest nicely on foam trays wrapped in plastic and probably back filled with nitrogen to help them maintain a more appealing color for longer. You almost don't even have to give much consideration to the animal from where each cut was harvested.

REMEMBER

For the most part, the protein that you can purchase at big-box retail stores or supermarkets is *commodity protein.* Commodity protein is mass produced, with efficiency and cost being the core drivers for all decision making. The animals have been bred to have specific genetic traits, raised intensively indoors to minimize external environmental variables, fed special diets intended to grow the animals to target weights more quickly, and processed in a manner to support shelf life through a national or international supply chain.

In 2019, the United States was estimated to import over 2.5 billion pounds of beef (https://www.ers.usda.gov/data-products/livestock-and-meat-international-trade-data/). These imports come from countries near and far, and are intended to keep up with the American appetite for animal protein on the cheap. Commodity protein, whether domestic or foreign in origin, is a cheap alternative to protein that is raised in the more traditional manner followed by many small family farms in the United States. Unfortunately, what you save in cost, you lose in quality.

SO GOD MADE A FARMER

And on the eighth day, God looked down on his planned paradise and said, "I need a caretaker." So God made a farmer.

God said, "I need somebody willing to get up before dawn, milk cows, work all day in the fields, milk cows again, eat supper and then go to town and stay past midnight at a meeting of the school board." So God made a farmer.

"I need somebody with arms strong enough to rustle a calf and yet gentle enough to deliver his own grandchild. Somebody to call hogs, tame cantankerous machinery, come home hungry, have to wait lunch until his wife's done feeding visiting ladies and tell the ladies to be sure and come back real soon — and mean it." So God made a farmer.

God said, "I need somebody willing to sit up all night with a newborn colt. And watch it die. Then dry his eyes and say, 'Maybe next year.' I need somebody who can shape an ax handle from a persimmon sprout, shoe a horse with a hunk of car tire, who can make harness out of haywire, feed sacks and shoe scraps. And who, planting time and harvest season, will finish his forty-hour week by Tuesday noon, then, pain'n from 'tractor back,' put in another seventy-two hours." So God made a farmer.

God had to have somebody willing to ride the ruts at double speed to get the hay in ahead of the rain clouds and yet stop in mid-field and race to help when he sees the first smoke from a neighbor's place. So God made a farmer.

God said, "I need somebody strong enough to clear trees and heave bails, yet gentle enough to tame lambs and wean pigs and tend the pink-combed pullets, who will stop his mower for an hour to splint the broken leg of a meadowlark. It had to be somebody who'd plow deep and straight and not cut corners. Somebody to seed, weed, feed, breed and rake and disc and plow and plant and tie the fleece and strain the milk and replenish the self-feeder and finish a hard week's work with a five-mile drive to church.

"Somebody who'd bale a family together with the soft strong bonds of sharing, who would laugh and then sigh, and then reply, with smiling eyes, when his son says he wants to spend his life 'doing what dad does.'" So God made a farmer. (Paul Harvey, "So God Made A Farmer," speech given at the 1978 FFA Conference)

Purchasing Protein from a Farmer

Farming isn't an easy profession to get into. It never has been, and no matter how much technology comes along, it never will be. It's a necessary labor of love, but, unfortunately, due to many factors — including government intervention, regulations written and sponsored by big business, and large-scale consolidation — the quintessentially American family farms are becoming fewer and farther between. If you want to get connected to your food, there is no better way than to purchase directly from a farm. There are many options today for doing this, whether through a CSA (community-supported agriculture) program, online grocery delivery services like MarketWagon.com, or your local farmers market.

One of the many benefits to purchasing protein directly from a farmer is that you can get all sorts of information on how the animals were raised, including the following:

>> You can find out where the animals were raised, whether the critters lived inside or outside, if they had space to move and root around or were confined, and so on.

>> You can learn about their diet. For example, did they get to forage for food or were they on a more controlled diet of different grains? You can also learn what kinds of grain they were raised on, whether or not they contained soy, corn, and so on, and whether the grain was GMO (genetically modified) or not.

>> You can determine whether or not the critters were on some sort of antibiotic or hormone regimen.

>> If the farm doesn't have an on-site processing plant, you can likely connect to the plant to learn how they process the animals and care for meat every step of the way.

I am of the opinion that knowing who is raising your food is better than just blindly purchasing something in a grocery store, even if it is labeled "free range" or "organic." In addition to knowing more about where and how the animals were raised, buying from a local farm keeps your dollars local, which helps the local farm employ neighbors, contributes toward local infrastructure, and so much more! Check out your local farmer's market to connect with local farmers. Farmers markets often run year round just like the Carmel Winter Farmers Market, in Indianapolis, pictured in Figure 3-1.

FIGURE 3-1:
Carmel Winter Farmers Market, Carmel, Indiana.

Mark LaFay

GUNTHORP FARMS

Greg Gunthorp is a fourth-generation hog farmer from northern Indiana. In the past 20 years, he and his growing family (three kids and now two grandkids) have managed to expand their small family hog business into a thriving operation that raises 120,000 chickens, 2,500 pigs, 10,000 turkeys, and 12,000 ducks annually, and processes them all in their on-site USDA-inspected processing facility. But what truly makes the Gunthorps stick out is that they've chosen to take a holistic approach to agriculture. Their animals are all pasture-raised. They rotate them across 270 acres of pasture, which allows the animals to graze and root around. The pigs are rotated across different pastures throughout the year, which allows them to eat down a section of earth; the roots die back and decompose, and then a new crop grows back up. This method of farming is known as *regenerative farming*, and it's catching on.

All of the improvements on their farm and in the processing plant are to get them closer and closer to being completely energy and resource independent so that the only thing they are really selling is sunshine! Greg (seen in the following figure) and his family are tirelessly working to redefine farming, and they aren't the only ones.

Photo by Kara Gunthorp

Another great benefit to supporting your local farmer is that it is better for the environment. You may have heard in the news about the issues in Brazil regarding the destruction of the rainforest. When you buy Brazilian beef, you are buying beef that is produced on rainforest wasteland, processed, and then boxed. The box is placed into a refrigerated diesel truck to be taken to a shipyard, where it is transferred to a refrigerated container on a diesel ocean freighter. The beef is then shipped several thousand miles up to an American port, where it is transferred from the boat to a holding area, where it is then transferred to a diesel truck to be shipped to a regional hub, where it is stored in refrigeration. The beef is then either further processed and re-packed, or just transferred to another diesel truck that then takes it to its destination. Once it arrives, it is then removed from its packaging, processed further, and put on the shelf.

Buying from your local farmer is much different. If your farmer does processing on site, the animal is walked to the processing plant, where it is dispatched, processed, packaged, and stored. The farmer loads up a refrigerated diesel truck and delivers to CSA, restaurants, and the farmers market where it is purchased. Seems much simpler, doesn't it?

Meat the Butcher

A long time ago, before the proliferation of supermarkets, the butcher shop was more than just a department in a store. A butcher shop was a brick-and-mortar location where you went to get all things meat! Butcher shops were generational family businesses, and with them came nuances that reflected the flavor and passion of the family. In Indianapolis, the oldest butcher shop is a German-owned business called Claus' German Sausage and Meats. If you're ever in town, it's worth a visit to sample the different authentic German recipes they still make and specialize in to this day!

In recent years there has been some renewal, a renaissance of sorts, within the field of craft butchery. A younger, energized generation of chefs, butchers, and culinary enthusiasts have started delving into whole animal butchery and opening a new (old) type of butcher shop, different from what you might find at the supermarket. These "artisanal" butcher shops and the creative people behind them have been instrumental in bridging the gap between the consumer and the small family farmer.

This new breed of butcher shop generally works closely with local farms to source heritage animal breeds, such as the one in Figure 3-2. These are breeds from long ago, before animals were hybridized beyond recognition of their genealogical origins. Different breeds have different qualities that make them desirable, including fat concentration and body placement, marbling within the muscles, consistency of protein and fat, and protein color. Chefs and butchers are also working with farmers to encourage different sorts of additions to the animals' diet, which also have a direct impact on the flavor of the meat. It's amazing how many wonderful things the farmer can do to impart quality to the meat!

FIGURE 3-2:
Large English
black hog.

Mark LaFay

TIP

A good butcher will be able to help you make proper meat selections for whatever your project may be. However, it is helpful to understand a little bit about the anatomy of pigs and cows because regional nuance can cause some confusion. For example, much of the whole-muscle charcuterie that I discuss in later chapters is based on cuts that are pretty typical for Italian butchers, but not as typical for American butchers.

One of the biggest issues I ran into when I first started tinkering in charcuterie was getting a coppa cut. *Coppa* is a muscle group that runs from the top of the shoulder (Boston butt) and into the neck. This muscle group is typically called a *collar.* American barbecue aficionados know it as "the money muscle." Familiarizing yourself with these nuances will be very helpful as you try to communicate the cuts you are looking for to your butcher. There's nothing worse than special ordering a cut, only to receive the wrong one and be stuck with it!

Working with Wild Game

What originally got me interested in meat processing, sausage making, charcuterie, and the like was hunting. I started hunting squirrels with my father when I was 12 years old, and I shot my first deer when I was 14. As an adult in my late twenties, I found my interest starting to turn into more of a passion. I love putting venison in the freezer. There is something about hunting, harvesting, and processing wild game that truly speaks to my primal core. But when it came to sharing wild venison with friends, sometimes I would get pushback because the venison tasted "gamey." I had personally never had an aversion to venison because I grew up eating it, but I can understand how someone might taste venison, especially venison that wasn't harvested appropriately, and think it tasted different from beef, which can often taste quite bland. Figure 3-3 is a picture of me with a white-tail deer taken in Illinois several years ago.

FIGURE 3-3:
Me with a nice
Midwestern
white-tail deer.

Mark LaFay

Venison and other wild game can acquire strong flavors that may be off-putting to others if the critter isn't harvested correctly. Following are several hunting tips to ensure your meat has the best flavor:

>> **Quick and clean kill.** Regardless of what you are hunting with, you want to have a one-shot kill through a vital region. This means head, heart, or lungs. The optimal would be a heart or head shot because the animal can expire

almost instantly. Quick kills are the most humane, and a quick kill reduces the chances the animal will pump a large amount of adrenaline and hormones into its blood before it dies. These two things can have a dramatic impact on the flavor of their meat.

>> **Gender.** This topic is considered very subjective by some. To me, however, personal experience has proven that if you are hunting for meat in the freezer, does (females) are a better option than bucks (males). This is because does are more tender and the testosterone in bucks can impart stronger flavors in their meat.

>> **Dressing.** When any animal is dispatched, the clock starts ticking to get the carcass cold. The sooner you do so, the faster you will slow down the decaying process. Deer and other wild game are no different. Field dress your animal immediately, and get the hide off as soon as you can.

REMEMBER

Equally as important to how you handle your animal in the field is how you handle it in the kitchen. Clean your meat, and remove all foreign material like shot, bullet shrapnel, hair, and any undesirable matter that may be present. If you aren't planning to further process your wild game into sausage or charcuterie, then you also need to package it well and freeze it until you are ready to use it. Vacuum sealing your meat scraps is the best way to ensure maximum quality.

Selecting Your Spices

Spices are the spice of life. Isn't that how the saying goes? One of the many aspects of charcuterie that I love is the diversity of flavors that can be found. Most regions of the world have their own flavor profile due to the herbs and spices that are readily available in their corner of the globe. You can find a lot of localized flavors in the charcuterie of an area, which can make this craft very fun for those who are adventurous. The rule of thumb, quality in equals quality out, applies very much to spices and other auxiliary ingredients for your recipes. Following are some tips for finding and using the best ingredients:

>> Spices and ingredients produced locally to your recipe are a great starting point. For example, if you are producing a recipe that calls for Calabrian chiles, don't settle for red pepper; look specifically for Calabrian chiles.

>> Purchase whole-seed spices. Even if your recipe calls for ground spices, purchase the whole seed and invest in a spice grinder. You will get a much fresher representation of the spice.

>> A little heat goes a long way. Warming a spice before you use it will wake up the oils and other flavor chemicals in the spice.

>> If your recipe calls for a toasted spice, toast it. Don't skip the extra step because you're feeling a little lazy.

You can easily find most spices on Amazon.com; a quick Google search will also reveal several good options. While purchasing spices at the grocery store isn't the worst option, it isn't the best either. The spices at the grocery store could be months, if not years, old. Plus, due to the volume, buying them will be far more expensive than buying in bulk.

TIP

Storing your spices in an airtight container is the best way to preserve their flavor for extended periods of time.

Salt of the earth

Salt is one seasoning that tends not to get much love from the general public. In fact, salt is usually regarded as a naughty spice because of its overuse in processed foods. Like all things, salt can also be toxic; for example, it was used in warfare as a way to destroy vast expanses of farmland. However, salt is also critical for bringing out flavor in our dishes. It has preserving and medicinal powers, and our bodies require salt to maintain homeostasis. In ancient cultures, it was used as currency, and medieval European villages were built around salt mines like the one shown in Figure 3-4.

FIGURE 3-4:
Ancient salt mine.

Even today, salt is a very important addition to any kitchen. In charcuterie it is critical for producing flavorful and safe products. Aside from the flavoring benefits of salt, it is critical for slowing the rate of spoilage in meat. One way that salt does this is by drawing water out of protein tissue. Bacteria need moisture to survive, and so reducing the amount of water available to bacteria is of paramount importance.

Several types of salt are available for use in the kitchen:

>> **Iodized salt.** Also referred to as "table salt," iodized salt is a fine-grain particle of salt that is blended with trace amounts of iodine. Iodine deficiency was at one time a common cause of defects in children in their developmental stages. Iodizing salt reduced this global problem. However, iodized salt is not ideal for charcuterie because the iodine can have a negative impact on the flavor of your products.

>> **Kosher salt.** Kosher salt is a large, flaked salt that is not iodized. Its shape and size are ideal for many volume-based recipes because you have less mass per volume measure. Kosher salt is a suitable option for charcuterie.

>> **Sea salt.** Salt that is extracted from ocean water is called sea salt. There are many ways to gather sea salt. One common method is through evaporation using large, open-air beds of water in fields (see Figure 3-5). Many higher-end French salts like Fleur de Sel are made in this manner. Sea salt can also be gathered by rapidly evaporating ocean water using heat. Sea salt is preferred because of its flavor and because it is the most natural form of salt. Many regional recipes may actually call for sea salt from the area due to its flavoring properties. All the recipes in this book call for sea salt.

FIGURE 3-5:
Sea salt
production.

© Getty Images/Malcolm Chapman/Contributor

Sodium nitrite / nitrate

Sodium nitrite is a potty word for most health-conscious folks, and this is due in part to the conflicting research on the health benefits and detriments of nitrates and nitrites. If you want to find research to support a stance that nitrates and nitrites are bad for you, that's pretty easy. Conversely, you can also find research in support of nitrates and nitrites. I won't get into the weeds on this topic, but instead will simply take the position that, as with all things, moderation is key.

So what are these nitrates and nitrites? Well, simply put, sodium nitrite is an inorganic compound that is found naturally in several root vegetables and dark-green leafy vegetables. It can also be found in the soil, and in some parts of the globe there are large concentrations of the chemical where it can actually be mined. Sodium nitrite's contribution to meat preparation is two-fold:

>> Sodium nitrite reacts with meat myoglobin to preserve the red or pink color in the meat after cooking.

>> The greatest value of sodium nitrite is that it inhibits the growth of botulism in meat. Botulism loves warm, anaerobic environments (little to no oxygen). One such environment is inside sausages and another is inside a smoker. Refrigerator temperatures can slow or stall the growth of botulism, so nitrates aren't a necessity in fresh sausages. They are, however, a must when producing salami that is fermented at 60 to 75 degrees Fahrenheit and then stored at or just below 55 degrees Fahrenheit. Nitrites are also a must for any meats that are smoked.

When you are making salami, you will use sodium nitrate because over time, it slowly breaks down into sodium nitrite; this slow breakdown controls the release of the nitrite over time. This is a beneficial quality for making dry-cured ground charcuterie.

When shopping for sodium nitrite, its common name is pink salt #1 (shown in Figure 3-6). Sodium nitrate is known as pink salt #2. Both salts are pink as a safety precaution so that they aren't mistaken for table salt. Pink salts #1 and #2 should not be mistaken for Himalayan pink salt, which is a fancy mineral salt and does not contain the required concentrations of sodium nitrite or nitrate.

Pink salts #1 and #2 are diluted forms of sodium nitrite and nitrate, respectively. They are typically diluted down to 6.25-percent concentration. The USDA requires that sodium nitrite / nitrate not exceed concentrations of 200 parts per million. To keep things simple and safe, all of the recipes in the later chapters of this book will be based on weights, so you will not have to learn how to calculate nitrite or nitrate concentrations.

Photo by David Pluimer

Celery juice powders

Have you ever noticed bacon, sausage, or salami that touts being "nitrate free"? This labeling isn't being 100-percent truthful. Here is the quick and dirty on this topic. Some vegetables contain high quantities of nitrites and nitrates, like beets, kale, celery, and mustard greens. If you want to produce a "nitrate-free" bacon or salami, one way is by using celery juice powder, which is a concentrated extraction of celery root. This extract powder contains nitrates in concentrations adequate for making bacon and salami. The USDA, however, requires that producers put "nitrate free" on the packaging. This is because nitrates weren't added; instead, celery juice powder, which contains the nitrates, was added.

I don't like vegetable juice powders in the place of proper sodium nitrite because the labeling is deceptive *and* because celery juice powder gives off a flavor that can be easily detected. Thus, all recipes in this book that call for nitrites or nitrates will ask for pink salt #1 or pink salt #2.

2

Making Meat Treats

IN THIS PART . . .

Make smoked bacon.

Grind, stuff, and link sausages.

Learn sausage recipes for all occasions.

Ferment and dry salamis.

Preserve meats by dry curing.

Chapter **4**

Fresh and Dry-Cured Whole Muscles

Bacon is proof God loves us and wants us to be happy.

— UNKNOWN

Several years ago my wife and I launched Old Major Market with a vision to produce artisanal sausages, bacons, and provisions. As I launched into the "how" of this endeavor, I thought, "Let's take the lean startup approach and identify our 'minimum viable product' and build from there." So I got to thinking, "What the heck is our minimum viable product?!" Naturally, we decided to start with the one thing that everyone loves: bacon. There was actually a study done on bacon consumption in America that found 90 percent of Americans ate bacon and the other ten percent of Americans were liars.

The love of bacon in America is undeniable. For many food enthusiasts who take the plunge into the wild world of charcuterie, the gateway drug is bacon. Bacon, relatively speaking, is a very approachable starting point and is a relatively safe product on which to cut your teeth. However, there is so much more to this journey than just hot-smoked bacons. Old World-style, dry-cured, whole-muscle charcuterie offers so many possibilities, especially as you explore different regional variations.

In this chapter you will learn about the differences between fresh-cured and dry-cured meats. You will also explore recipes for several types of hot-smoked bacon, Italian-inspired recipes for dry curing different cuts of pork and beef, and recipes for curing fish.

Fresh-Cured Bacons

To put it simply, fresh bacon is pork belly that is rubbed down with a mixture of salt, sugar, and sodium nitrite (pink salt). The pork belly is then refrigerated for one to two weeks, after which it is hot smoked until its internal temperature is 145 degrees Fahrenheit. The mixture of salt, sugar, and pink salt is the "cure," and the bacon is considered to be "fresh" because it must be stored at refrigeration and has a finite shelf life.

Curing is a slow process whereby the salts and sugars slowly work their way through the cells of the protein through a process called *osmosis*. Curing can take a few days to several weeks, depending on the size and thickness of the cut of meat.

REMEMBER

The recipes in this chapter all utilize a process known as *equilibrium curing*, or EQ curing. EQ curing is a precise way of measuring salt, sugar, and nitrite by percentage of mass of the protein being cured; this method allows you to completely control the amount of salt in your products. When a cut of meat is curing, it can stay in refrigeration for some time because the salt and nitrite dramatically slow the replication rate of spoilage bacteria.

Hot smoking serves multiple purposes:

>> Flavoring the meat with smoke. Different woods impart different flavors. Popular woods for smoking include hickory, cherry, pecan, maple, apple, alder, and oak.

>> Killing off all bacteria by raising the internal temperature to a target temperature for a prescribed amount of time.

>> Partial drying by rapidly evaporating water during the cooking process.

>> Enhancing the texture through cooking.

When hot smoking bacon, you are fully cooking it. Could you eat your own bacon without cooking it in the pan to crisp it up? Sure! But I wouldn't suggest trying that with anyone else's bacon.

Smoked Belly Bacon

PREP TIME: 15 MINUTES	CURING TIME: 7 DAYS	YIELD: 4 LBS.

INGREDIENTS

34 grams (1.5%) sea salt

17 grams (.75%) white sugar

6 grams (.25%) pink salt #1

5 lbs. pork belly (skin off)

1 food-safe plastic bag

1 black Sharpie marker

1 Combine the dry ingredients in a mixing bowl to make the EQ cure mixture.

2 Place the pork belly in the plastic bag.

3 With the bag open, ensure the belly is flat on your work surface, protein side up.

4 Sprinkle approximately 70 percent of the EQ cure mixture on the protein side of the pork belly.

5 Rub the EQ cure mixture into the pork belly, being sure to evenly coat the entire protein side.

6 Leave the pork belly in the bag, and flip it over so that it is fat side up.

7 Sprinkle the remaining EQ cure mixture over the fat side of the pork belly.

8 Rub the EQ cure mixture into the pork belly, being sure to evenly coat the entire fat side.

9 Wrap the pork belly in the bag, being sure to get as much air out as possible.

10 Lay the wrapped pork belly in your refrigerator, making sure that it is lying flat.

11 Wait at least 7 days.

12 Remove the pork belly from the bag and rinse it under cold water.

13 Pat the pork belly dry with single-use paper towels.

14 Let the pork belly rest on a cooling rack in the fridge overnight. This will allow the pork belly to slightly dry out and form a pellicle.

(continued)

15 Place the pork belly in a smoker at 180–225 degrees Fahrenheit. Apply constant smoke to the pork belly for the duration of the cooking process.

16 After 2 hours, check the internal temperature of the pork belly by inserting a digital temperature probe. Check the temperature every 45–60 minutes until the temperature in the middle of the pork belly reaches 145 degrees Fahrenheit.

17 Once the pork belly has reached an internal temperature of 145 degrees Fahrenheit, remove it and place it on a cooling rack in a cool area in your kitchen.

18 Once the pork belly has cooled below 100 degrees Fahrenheit, place it on a cooling rack in your refrigerator and cool it overnight.

19 Once the pork belly has cooled below 41 degrees Fahrenheit, slice it. I prefer to do this on a meat slicer for uniformity; however, if you do not have one, you can use a knife and cutting board.

TIP: If your protein has a different weight than the prescribed weight in the recipe, update the recipe by using the percentages provided. Multiply the mass of your protein (in grams) by the percent of the ingredient. This will provide the mass of the ingredient in grams.

TIP: Smoke using a mixture of cherry and hickory.

TIP: A pellicle is a slightly dry rind on the outside of your meat. Smoke will not stick to water, so it is important to dry your pork belly out before smoking. However, you can skip this step if you are in a hurry; the pork belly will dry in the smoker. Note that the end product will not be as smoky as it would if you let it dry a little prior to smoking.

TIP: Using your Sharpie, write on the bag the date the pork belly went into your fridge to cure and the date it can be removed to smoke.

VARY IT! Try different woods to get different smoke flavors. Apple is a great mild flavor.

WARNING: Cooling hot meat quickly is important. Be sure to use cooling racks, and don't try to cool it in sealed containers. Use a fan if you want to speed up the cooling process. The USDA recommends that meat containing nitrites be cooled from 130°F to 80°F in 5 hours or less and from 80° to 45°F in 10 hours or less.

Maple Bacon

PREP TIME: 15 MINUTES	CURING TIME: 7 DAYS	YIELD: 4 LBS.

INGREDIENTS

34 grams (1.5%) sea salt

17 grams (.75%) white sugar

68 grams (3%) brown sugar

6 grams (.25%) pink salt #1

5 lbs. pork belly (skin off)

1 food-safe plastic bag

1 black Sharpie marker

1   Combine the dry ingredients in a mixing bowl to make the EQ cure mixture (with added brown sugar).

2   Place the pork belly in the plastic bag.

3   With the bag open, ensure the pork belly is flat on your work surface, protein side up.

4   Sprinkle approximately 70 percent of the EQ cure mixture on the protein side of the pork belly.

5   Rub the EQ cure mixture into the pork belly, being sure to evenly coat the entire protein side.

6   Leave the pork belly in the bag and flip it over so that it is fat side up.

7   Sprinkle the remaining EQ cure mixture over the fat side of the pork belly.

8   Rub the EQ cure mixture into the pork belly, being sure to evenly coat the entire fat side.

9   Wrap the pork belly in the bag, being sure to get as much air out as possible.

10   Lay the wrapped pork belly in your refrigerator, making sure that it is lying flat.

11   Wait at least 7 days.

12   Remove the pork belly from the bag and rinse it under cold water.

13   Pat the pork belly dry with single-use paper towels.

(continued)

14 Let the pork belly rest on a cooling rack in the fridge over-night. This will allow the pork belly to slightly dry out and form a pellicle.

15 Place the pork belly in a smoker at 180–225 degrees Fahrenheit. Apply constant maple smoke to the pork belly for the duration of the cooking process.

16 After 2 hours, check the internal temperature of the pork belly by inserting a digital temperature probe. Check the temperature every 45–60 minutes until the temperature in the middle of the pork belly reaches 145 degrees Fahrenheit.

17 Once the pork belly has reached an internal temperature of 145 degrees Fahrenheit, remove it and place it on a cooling rack in a cool area in your kitchen.

18 Once the pork belly has cooled below 100 degrees Fahrenheit, place it on a cooling rack in your refrigerator and cool it overnight.

19 Once the pork belly has cooled below 41 degrees Fahrenheit, slice it. I prefer to do this on a meat slicer for uniformity; however, if you do not have one, you can use a knife and cutting board.

TIP: If your protein has a different weight than the prescribed weight in the recipe, update the recipe by using the percentages provided. Multiply the mass of your protein (in grams) by the percent of the ingredient. This will provide the mass of the ingredient in grams.

TIP: Smoke using a mixture of cherry and hickory.

TIP: A pellicle is a slightly dry rind on the outside of your meat. Smoke will not stick to water, so it is important to dry your pork belly out before smoking. However, you can skip this step if you are in a hurry; the pork belly will dry in the smoker. Note that the end product will not be as smoky as it would if you let it dry a little prior to smoking.

TIP: Using your Sharpie, write on the bag the date the pork belly went into your fridge to cure and the date it can be removed to smoke.

WARNING: Cooling hot meat quickly is important. Be sure to use cooling racks, and don't try to cool it in sealed containers. Use a fan if you want to speed up the cooling process. The USDA recommends that meat containing nitrites be cooled from 130°F to 80°F in 5 hours or less and from 80°F to 45°F in 10 hours or less.

Jowl Bacon

PREP TIME: 15 MINUTES	CURING TIME: 7 DAYS	YIELD: 4 LBS.

INGREDIENTS

7 grams (1.5%) sea salt

4 grams (.75%) white sugar

1 gram (.25%) pink salt #1

18 grams (4%) coarse ground black pepper

18 grams (4%) coarse ground coriander

1 lb. pork jowl (skin off)

1 food-safe plastic bag

1 black Sharpie marker

1 Combine the dry ingredients in a mixing bowl to make the EQ cure mixture (with added spices).

2 Place the pork jowl in the plastic bag.

3 With the bag open, ensure the pork jowl is flat on your work surface, protein side up.

4 Sprinkle approximately 70 percent of the EQ cure mixture on the protein side of the pork jowl.

5 Rub the EQ cure mixture into the pork jowl, being sure to evenly coat the entire protein side.

6 Leave the pork jowl in the bag and flip it over so that is fat side up.

7 Sprinkle the remaining EQ cure mixture over the fat side of the pork jowl.

8 Rub the EQ cure mixture into the pork jowl, being sure to evenly coat the entire fat side.

9 Wrap the pork jowl in the bag, being sure to get as much air out as possible.

10 Lay the wrapped pork jowl in your refrigerator, making sure that it is lying flat.

11 Wait at least 7 days.

12 Remove the pork jowl from the bag. Don't rinse it.

13 Let the pork jowl rest on a cooling rack in the fridge overnight. This will allow the pork jowl to slightly dry out and form a pellicle.

(continued)

14 Place the pork jowl in a smoker at 180–225 degrees Fahrenheit. Apply constant smoke to the pork jowl for the duration of the cooking process.

15 After 2 hours, check the internal temperature of the pork jowl by inserting a digital temperature probe in the thickest part. Check the temperature every 45–60 minutes until the temperature reaches 145 degrees Fahrenheit.

16 Once the pork jowl has reached an internal temperature of 145 degrees Fahrenheit, remove it and place it on a cooling rack in a cool area in your kitchen.

17 Once the pork jowl has cooled below 100 degrees Fahrenheit, place it on a cooling rack in your refrigerator and cool it overnight.

18 Once the pork jowl has cooled below 41 degrees Fahrenheit, slice it. I prefer to do this on a meat slicer for uniformity; however, if you do not have one, you can use a knife and cutting board.

TIP: If your protein has a different weight than the prescribed weight in the recipe, update the recipe by using the percentages provided. Multiply the mass of your protein (in grams) by the percent of the ingredient. This will provide the mass of the ingredient in grams.

TIP: Smoke using a mixture of cherry and hickory.

TIP: A pellicle is a slightly dry rind on the outside of your meat. Smoke will not stick to water, so it is important to dry your pork jowl out before smoking. However, you can skip this step if you are in a hurry; the pork jowl will dry in the smoker. Note that the end product will not be as smoky as it would if you let it dry a little prior to smoking.

TIP: Using your Sharpie, write on the bag the date the pork jowl went into your fridge to cure and the date it can be removed to smoke.

WARNING: Cooling hot meat quickly is important. Be sure to use cooling racks, and don't try to cool it in sealed containers. Use a fan if you want to speed up the cooling process. The USDA recommends that meat containing nitrites be cooled from 130°F to 80°F in 5 hours or less and from 80°F to 45°F in 10 hours or less.

Smoked Rasher Bacon

PREP TIME: 15 MINUTES	CURING TIME: 7 DAYS	YIELD: 4 LBS.

INGREDIENTS

34 grams (1.5%) sea salt

17 grams (.75%) white sugar

6 grams (.25%) pink salt #1

5 lbs. pork loin with 2–3 inches of the pork side still attached

1 food-safe plastic bag

1 black Sharpie marker

1 Combine the dry ingredients in a mixing bowl to make the EQ cure mixture.

2 Place the pork loin in the plastic bag.

3 With the bag open, ensure the pork loin is flat on your work surface, protein side up.

4 Sprinkle approximately 50 percent of the EQ cure mixture on the protein side of the pork loin.

5 Rub the EQ cure mixture into the pork loin, being sure to evenly coat the entire protein side.

6 Leave the pork loin in the bag and flip it over so that it is fat side up.

7 Sprinkle the remaining EQ cure mixture over the fat side of the pork loin.

8 Rub the EQ cure mixture into the pork loin, being sure to evenly coat the entire fat side.

9 Wrap the pork loin in the bag, being sure to get as much air out as possible.

10 Lay the wrapped pork loin in your refrigerator, making sure that it is lying flat.

11 Wait at least 10 days.

12 Remove the pork loin from the bag and rinse it under cold water.

13 Pat the pork loin dry with single-use paper towels.

14 Let the pork loin rest on a cooling rack in the fridge over-night. This will allow the pork loin to slightly dry out and form a pellicle.

(continued)

15 Place the pork loin in a smoker at 180–225 degrees Fahrenheit. Apply constant smoke to it for the duration of the cooking process.

16 After 2 hours, check the internal temperature of the pork loin by inserting a digital temperature probe into the middle of the thickest part. Check the temperature every 45–60 minutes until the temperature reaches 145 degrees Fahrenheit.

17 Once the pork loin has reached an internal temperature of 145 degrees Fahrenheit, remove it and place it on a cooling rack in a cool area in your kitchen.

18 Once the pork loin has cooled below 100 degrees Fahrenheit, place it on a cooling rack in your refrigerator and cool it overnight.

19 Once the pork loin has cooled below 41 degrees Fahrenheit, slice it. I prefer to do this on a meat slicer for uniformity; however, if you do not have one, you can use a knife and cutting board.

TIP: If your protein has a different weight than the prescribed weight in the recipe, update the recipe by using the percentages provided. Multiply the mass of your protein (in grams) by the percent of the ingredient. This will provide the mass of the ingredient in grams.

TIP: Smoke using a mixture of cherry and hickory.

TIP: A pellicle is a slightly dry rind on the outside of your meat. Smoke will not stick to water, so it is important to dry your pork loin out before smoking. However, you can skip this step if you are in a hurry; the pork loin will dry in the smoker. Note that the end product will not be as smoky as it would if you let it dry a little prior to smoking.

TIP: Using your Sharpie, write on the bag the date the pork loin went into your fridge to cure and the date it can be removed to smoke.

VARY IT! Try different woods to get different smoke flavors. Apple is a great mild flavor.

WARNING: Cooling hot meat quickly is important. Be sure to use cooling racks, and don't try to cool it in sealed containers. Use a fan if you want to speed up the cooling process. The USDA recommends that meat containing nitrites be cooled from 130°F to 80°F in 5 hours or less and from 80°F to 45°F in 10 hours or less.

Dry-Cured Meats

The Old World technique of dry curing meats was once used out of necessity to preserve the various parts of an animal that couldn't be consumed before they spoiled. However, today dry curing is done because this technique produces absolutely wonderful meats with incredible flavors and textures. If you've never had guanciale that has been dry cured and aged for six months, you haven't lived! The fat melts in your mouth like some sort of out-of-this-world savory pork candy!

Dry curing takes a great deal of time and patience. It also requires some specialized equipment so that you can control environmental variables that will impact the quality and safety of your product.

Dry-curing chambers are critical for making dry-cured meats. Find out where to purchase one or how to build one by referring to Chapter 1.

REMEMBER

Minding mold

When I was growing up, if there was mold on some cheese in the fridge, my dad would tell us to cut it off and keep eating. In a way it seemed gross, but in reality he was right; the mold on the cheese was only on the surface, and once it was removed, the cheese was fine to eat. Mold is an environmental variable that, if not managed, can become a real pain in the butt. But not all mold is bad. Did you know that the antibiotic called penicillin comes from a particular type of mold? Mold from the Penicillium family is often found growing on dry-cured meats and aged cheeses. In fact, salamis (see Figure 4-1) can, and often should, be inoculated with these molds as a protection against bad molds. (More on this in Chapter 7.)

As a general rule, white molds that are dusty and not puffy or fuzzy are considered safe. Any other color of mold is bad news and should be cleaned off with distilled vinegar as soon as it is noticed. When you work with meat, you will encounter mold. Don't worry, though; there are several ways to protect yourself against mold:

>> Use proper hygiene and sanitation when prepping your products.

>> Sanitize your dry-curing chamber by wiping all surfaces down with vinegar and single-use towels.

>> After washing your hands, put on single-use food handler gloves.

>> Never touch the product with bare hands while it is drying.

>> Minimize opening your dry-curing chamber once it is loaded with product.

FIGURE 4-1:
Salami coated
with white
Penicillium mold.

Mark LaFay

TIP

If you are unsure about the mold on your meat products, clean it off with vinegar and single-use towels.

REMEMBER

Before you handle meat, wash your hands, clean and sanitize your work area, and put on single-use food handler gloves.

Drying to preserve

Drying meat reduces the amount of water in protein tissue. This is done to preserve or extend the life of the protein. All bacteria require water to survive and replicate. Removing water is necessary to eliminate these bacteria, which can spoil your products and make you sick. You can also control water content by salting. The recipes and procedures for dry curing meats in this book use a combination of salt and drying to control water activity.

Controlling temperature and humidity is of paramount importance when dry curing. Your drying temperature should be between 50 and 55 degrees Fahrenheit; don't deviate from this. Your environment should be dry as well, but not too dry. If your environment is too dry, your products will dry too rapidly, causing hardening of the outsides and slowing the drying of the insides. If your environment is too humid, your products will take too long to dry, or may not dry at all. Drying at 70 to 75 percent relative humidity is an ideal range.

Dry-curing chambers have all of these controls built in and automatically managed. If you aren't using a dry-curing chamber, then you can monitor the humidity with a small digital hydrometer (humidity meter), and the temperature with a digital thermometer, both of which you can purchase on Amazon.com.

Water activity can be approximated by calculating percent weight loss using this formula:

1 – (finished weight / starting weight) = percent weight loss

As a general rule, you want to achieve a minimum of 30 percent weight loss during drying. The more weight the meat loses, the firmer the final product becomes. Fatty products like guanciale may not lose 30 percent because there is less available water in fat.

Each recipe will provide a target percent weight loss. However, if you are still concerned with the level of drying, you can calculate your water activity with an activity meter. Pathogenic bacterial growth is not supported at water activity (a_w) of .85 or less, so this is a desirable minimum to attain for safety.

Tying the knot

I would imagine that sailors make the best charcutiers because of the many knots they know how to tie. Your meats will be hung in the dry-curing chamber so that they are not in contact with any products or surfaces for the duration of the drying process. This is to ensure proper airflow for drying and to reduce potential spoilage during drying. There are several different ways to tie up your products so they can be hung, and in some cases to form the cuts so they take on a specific shape while drying. The only knot you will need to know for the recipes in the next few sections is similar to a square knot. Follow these steps (you can also refer to Figure 4-2):

1. **Draw the string so that it is under the coppa.**

2. **Bring the string up on both sides of the coppa.**

3. **Cross the string over itself to make an "x."**

4. **Wrap one end over the other end three times.**

5. **Carefully pull each end of the string to cinch down the string.**

6. **One last time, bring the ends of the string together to form an "x."**

7. **Wrap one end over the other side one time, and pull it tight to complete the knot.**

TIP

This knot is very useful for making charcuterie because it tends not to slip when you tie it off. There are several other ways to tie up your products; however, I will default to this simple method for the purposes of this book.

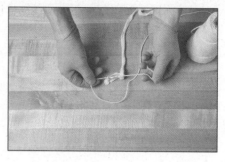

FIGURE 4-2:
Knot-tying steps.

Photos by David Pluimer

Documenting details

When you are making dry-cured meats, a lot of time will pass from when you start to when you finish. Make sure you don't forget any critical details by documenting everything as you go. A tried-and-true method for doing this is with small hang tags. Here is a list of what you should document on your product hang tags:

>> Name of the product

>> Date the product went into the dry-curing chamber

>> Weight of the product in grams when it went into the dry-curing chamber

>> Recipe (just record the ingredients and their percentages)

>> Date the product came out of the dry-curing chamber to be weighed

>> [Weight of the product when it was weighed] + [percent of weight loss]

TIP

Place the hang tag on the hook or strings used to hang the product in your dry-curing chamber. This will make your life much easier as you check in on your sleeping meat treats throughout the year!

Pancetta Tesa (Flat Pancetta)

PREP TIME: 30 MINUTES	CURE TIME: 14 DAYS	DRY TIME: APPROXIMATELY 60–120 DAYS	TARGET WEIGHT LOSS: 35 PERCENT

INGREDIENTS

(3%) sea salt

(.25%) pink salt #1

(.5%) coarse ground juniper berry

(.5%) red pepper flake

(.5%) coarse ground coriander

(.25%) dry rosemary

(1%) crushed fresh garlic clove

(.13%) crumbled bay leaf

Pork belly, skin off

1 food-safe plastic bag

1 Weigh your pork belly and convert the weight into grams.

2 Calculate the ingredient weights by multiplying the weight of the pork belly by the percent provided for each ingredient.

3 Combine the ingredients in a mixing bowl.

4 Place the pork belly in a food-safe plastic bag, protein side up.

5 Apply approximately 50 percent of the seasoning mixture to the protein side and rub it into the tissue, being sure to cover the entire surface.

6 Leave the pork belly in the bag, and flip it over so that it is fat side up.

7 Apply the remaining seasoning mixture to the fat side, being sure to cover the entire surface.

8 Wrap the pork belly in the bag, being sure to remove as much as air as possible.

9 Lay the pork belly flat in your refrigerator and leave it to cure for 14 days.

10 Remove the pork belly from the refrigerator and run a meat "S" hook through one corner of the pork belly.

(continued)

11 Hang the pork belly in your dry-curing chamber to dry at a temperature between 50 and 60 degrees Fahrenheit, and a humidity between 60 and 65 percent.

12 After 60 days, remove the hanging pork belly from the dry-curing chamber. Weigh it and calculate the weight loss percent using the formula provided earlier in the section, "Drying to preserve." If the target weight loss hasn't been reached, let the pancetta continue drying in the dry-curing chamber. Check again in two weeks.

13 Once the pancetta has reached the target weight loss, cut it into small chunks and vacuum pack each piece individually. I suggest you store them in the fridge, as this will ensure higher flavor quality much longer.

TIP: If you don't have a dry-curing chamber, you can always try hanging the pancetta in a dark, cool spot in your basement.

TIP: Curing your pancetta in a vacuum-sealed bag will speed the process and reduce premature oxidation.

Guanciale

PREP TIME: 30 MINUTES	CURE TIME: 14 DAYS	DRY TIME: APPROXIMATELY 60–120 DAYS	TARGET WEIGHT LOSS: 30 PERCENT

INGREDIENTS

(3%) sea salt

(.25%) pink salt #1

(1%) coarse ground black pepper

(.5%) coarse ground juniper berry

(.5%) red pepper flake

(.5%) coarse ground coriander

(1%) crushed fresh garlic clove

Pork jowl, skin off

1 food-safe plastic bag

1 Weigh your pork jowl and convert the weight into grams.

2 Calculate the ingredient weights by multiplying the weight of the pork jowl by the percentage provided for each ingredient.

3 Combine the ingredients in a mixing bowl.

4 Place the pork jowl in a food-safe plastic bag, protein side up.

5 Apply approximately 50 percent of the seasoning mixture to the protein side and rub it into the tissue, being sure to cover the entire surface.

6 Leave the pork jowl in the bag, and flip it so that it is fat side up.

7 Apply the remaining seasoning mixture to the fat side, being sure to cover the entire surface.

8 Wrap the pork jowl in the bag, being sure to remove as much as air as possible.

9 Lay the pork jowl flat in your refrigerator and leave it to cure for 14 days.

10 Remove the pork jowl from the refrigerator and run a meat "S" hook through the thin end of the pork jowl.

11 Hang the pork jowl in your dry-curing chamber to dry at a temperature between 50 and 60 degrees Fahrenheit and a humidity between 60 and 65 percent.

(continued)

12 After 60 days, remove the hanging pork jowl from the dry-curing chamber. Weigh it and calculate the weight loss percent using the formula provided earlier in the section, "Drying to preserve." If the target percent weight loss hasn't been reached, let the guanciale continue drying in the dry–curing chamber. Check again in two weeks.

13 Once the guanciale has reached the target weight loss, vacuum pack it whole and store it in the fridge until you are ready to use it. If you don't have a vacuum sealer, wrap it in plastic wrap and store it in a Ziploc bag.

TIP: If you don't have a dry-curing chamber, you can always try hanging the guanciale in a dark, cool spot in your basement.

TIP: Curing your guanciale in a vacuum-sealed bag will speed the process and reduce premature oxidation.

TIP: Due to the fat content of pork jowls, the drying process can be much slower and you may not hit 30 percent weight loss. If after 90 days you have not reached 30 percent weight loss, the jowl may not loose any more. Take it down and give it a slice.

Coppa

PREP TIME: 30 MINUTES	CURE TIME: 14 DAYS	DRY TIME: APPROXIMATELY 60–120 DAYS	TARGET WEIGHT LOSS: 35 PERCENT

INGREDIENTS

(3%) sea salt

(.25%) pink salt #1

(.5%) coarse ground black pepper

(.25%) coarse ground juniper berry

(.25%) crumbled whole hop cones

(.4%) coarse ground coriander

(.125%) crumbled bay leaf

Pork coppa (also known as pork collar, or money muscle)

1 food-safe plastic bag

1 Weigh the pork and convert the weight into grams.

2 Calculate the ingredient weights by multiplying the weight of the pork by the percent provided for each ingredient.

3 Combine the ingredients in a mixing bowl.

4 Place the pork in a food-safe plastic bag; if you have a vacuum sealer, use a vacuum bag.

5 Evenly apply the seasoning mixture to each side of the pork.

6 With the pork in the bag, remove as much as air as possible, or vacuum seal it if you are using a vacuum bag.

7 Cure the pork in the refrigerator for 14 days.

8 Remove the cured pork from the refrigerator and tie it to compress and form the coppa. Tie it using the basic knot described earlier in the section, "Tying the knot." Tie your first knot 1 inch from the end of the coppa. Then tie additional knots every inch. Make sure that you cinch the knots tight to compress the coppa. When you tie your last knot, do not trim the string; instead, tie it off to form a loop to hang it with.

9 Hang the coppa in your dry-curing chamber to dry at a temperature between 50 and 60 degrees Fahrenheit and a humidity between 60 and 65 percent.

10 After 30 days, remove the hanging coppa from the dry-curing chamber. Weigh it and calculate the weight loss percent using the formula provided earlier in the section, "Drying to preserve." If the target percent weight loss hasn't been reached, let the coppa continue drying in the dry-curing chamber. Check again in two weeks.

(continued)

11 Once the coppa has reached the target weight loss, vacuum pack it whole and store it in the fridge for 30 to 60 days. This will allow any available moisture to even out and soften the outside of the coppa, which will likely have hardened during drying. If you don't have a vacuum sealer, tightly wrap it in plastic wrap and store it in a Ziploc bag.

12 Slice the coppa as you eat it. Do not slice it for storage, as it will oxidize and taste like bland pork.

TIP: If you don't have a dry-curing chamber, you can always try hanging the coppa in a dark, cool spot in your basement.

VARY IT! Try different spices in different quantities to achieve a variety of results.

Bresaola

PREP TIME: 30 MINUTES	CURE TIME: 14 DAYS	DRY TIME: APPROXIMATELY 60–120 DAYS	TARGET WEIGHT LOSS: 35–40 PERCENT

INGREDIENTS

(3%) sea salt

(.25%) pink salt #1

(.5%) coarse ground black pepper

Beef eye round (trimmed to be no more than 3–4 inches thick)

1 food-safe plastic bag

1 Weigh the beef and convert the weight into grams.

2 Calculate the ingredient weights by multiplying the weight of the beef by the percent provided for each ingredient.

3 Combine the ingredients in a mixing bowl.

4 Place the beef in a food-safe plastic bag; if you have a vacuum sealer, use a vacuum bag.

5 Evenly apply the seasoning mixture to each side of the beef.

6 Wrap the beef in the plastic bag, being sure to remove as much as air as possible; if you have a vacuum sealer, use a vacuum bag.

7 Cure the beef in the refrigerator for 14 days.

8 Remove the cured beef from the refrigerator and tie it to compress and form the bresaola. Tie it using the basic knot described earlier in the section, "Tying the knot." Tie your first knot 1 inch from the end of the bresaola. Then tie additional knots every inch. Make sure that you cinch the knots tight to compress the bresaola. When you tie your last knot, do not trim the string; instead, tie it off to form a loop to hang it with.

9 Hang the bresaola in your dry-curing chamber to dry at a temperature between 50 and 60 degrees Fahrenheit and a humidity between 60 and 65 percent.

10 After 30 days, remove the hanging bresaola from the dry-curing chamber. Weigh it and calculate the weight loss percent using the formula provided earlier in the section, "Drying to preserve." If the target percent weight loss hasn't been reached, let the bresaola continue drying in the dry-curing chamber. Check again in two weeks.

(continued)

11 Once the bresaola has reached the target weight loss, vacuum pack it whole and store it in the fridge for 30 to 60 days. This will allow any available moisture to even out and soften the outside of the bresaola, which will likely have hardened during drying. If you don't have a vacuum sealer, tightly wrap it in plastic wrap and store it in a Ziploc bag.

12 Slice the bresaola as you eat it. Do not slice it for storage, as it will oxidize and taste like bland meat.

TIP: If you don't have a dry-curing chamber, you can always try hanging the bresaola in a dark, cool spot in your basement.

VARY IT! Try different spices in different quantities to achieve a variety of results.

Curing Seafood

I love seafood of all forms. Cook it. Serve it raw. Salt it. Smoke it. You name it, I love seafood. When I was very young, my mother would feed us kids all different types of food. I remember eating paté and caviar as an eight year old. My brother's favorite meal as a kid for his birthday was cheese soufflé. One of the things my mom turned us on to was smoked nova salmon. A source of confusion is the difference between gravlax, lox, and nova. So let's clear that up!

» *Gravlax* is a Scandinavian-style cured salmon that is cured with salt, sugar, and fresh dill. You can also use other aromatics like citrus, gin, and beet juice to make it bright red.

» *Lox* is derived from a Yiddish word for 'salmon' and is traditionally made from salmon belly, which is wildly fatty. The belly is cured with salt and some sugar.

» *Nova* is very similar to lox, but it is made with the loin, not the belly, of salmon from Nova Scotia (you can make it from any salmon, though). It is cured with salt and some sugar and then cold smoked. *Cold smoking* is smoking without heat. Technically, it means smoking at temperatures under 100 degrees Fahrenheit. Smoking nova is better when done at temperatures below 50 degrees Fahrenheit.

WARNING

Gravlax, lox, and nova are all uncooked forms of salmon. To be safe when making these delicious bites, make sure that you practice proper hygiene and sanitation, as discussed in Chapter 2. Fish can be hosts for parasites that can wreak havoc on humans. To address this, freeze your fish below −4 degrees Fahrenheit for seven days. This will destroy any parasites and their eggs that may be present. Then you don't have to worry about going on the worm weight loss program.

Gravlax, Lox, Nova

INGREDIENTS

500 grams sea salt

250 grams sugar

100 grams fresh dill fronds (for gravlax only)

Salmon, skin off

1 On a small baking sheet, lay down three layers of plastic wrap long enough to cover your salmon.

2 In a mixing bowl, mix the sea salt and sugar.

3 Sprinkle a layer of the salt-and-sugar mixture on the plastic wrap, thick enough that you can't see through it.

4 Lay the salmon fillet (with the skin off) on the bed of salt and sugar.

5 (Gravlax only) Sprinkle the dill all over the top of the salmon.

6 Cover the salmon with the salt-and-sugar mixture.

7 Fold the plastic wrap over the salmon.

8 Place the baking sheet with the salmon into the refrigerator.

9 Place another baking sheet on top of the salmon and put a couple of weights on top of the baking sheet. A single brick will work nicely.

10 After 48 hours, remove the salmon from the fridge, and unwrap and rinse it.

11 Pat the salmon dry with single-use towels. For gravlax and lox, stop here and start eating. For nova, keep going.

12 Place the salmon on a cooling rack and return it to the fridge uncovered for 12 to 24 hours.

Unless you have fancy cold-smoking gear, you will have to cold smoke when the temperatures overnight are below 45 degrees Fahrenheit. Colder is better as long as it is not cold enough to freeze the fish. If you do not have a cold smoke generator, you can make one with an electric hot plate, a small cast–iron pan, and tin foil. Place the hot plate in your grill or smoker (you can even do this in a large cardboard box). Fill the cast–iron pan with wood chips and then wrap the pan in foil. Poke several holes in the foil. Turn the burner on low (low enough to slowly smolder the wood chips).

13 Place the cooling rack with salmon into your smoker. Be sure the temperature does not get above 45 degrees Fahrenheit, and smoke it for 12 hours.

14 After 12 hours, wrap the salmon in plastic wrap and return it to the fridge to cool.

15 Slice and eat!

TIP: Simplify the cold-smoking process by purchasing a cold smoke generator online.

TIP: If you want to make the salmon less salty, reduce the time it sits in the fridge curing.

VARY IT! Add different whole spices to the salmon to give it different flavors. For example, coat the lox with coriander and black pepper to make salmon pastrami!

Chapter **5**

Grinding and Stuffing Sausage

Laws are like sausages. It is better not to see them being made.
— OTTO VON BISMARCK

I don't know about laws, but making sausage is a pretty amazing activity. Hopefully you are interested in more than just watching the sausage being made, but actually participating! To the layperson, sausage is quite possibly as suspect as the mystery meat loaf one used to be served in the school cafeteria. But the reality is that sausage was born out of necessity (aren't all great things conceived that way?). Sausages are a wonderful way to utilize the different bits and pieces of an animal that are remaining once the main cuts, like steaks, chops, ribs, and so on, are processed and packaged. Even the offal (pronounced 'ah-full'), liver, heart, and kidney can be put to use in sausages. Waste not, want not!

One thing I love about sausage making is that it gives me the opportunity to showcase a little culinary creativity. Don't get me wrong; there are many ways within the craft of butchery that you can showcase both creativity and talent. With sausage, however, you have a blank canvas and a vast palette of options. Maybe it's the larger industrial sausage makers that have created a bad impression for the consumer. Industrial sausage making tends to rely on fillers, water retention, preservatives, and questionable protein sources. Industrial-scale food production is generally not about quality, but commodity. Cost and speed to market are the drivers. That sounds like a curtain I wouldn't want to look behind!

Home-crafted sausages, however, are fascinating because they come in so many shapes, sizes, textures, and flavors. Whether it's a coarsely ground Wisconsin-style bratwurst, a smooth, tender, smoky hot dog, or a slightly salty and funky dry-cured salami, there is a sausage for every occasion!

Grinding Sausages!

Meat grinders are machines designed specifically to break pieces of meat and fat into smaller pieces by forcing through a metal plate with several small holes. Sausage in its most basic iteration is simply ground meat with seasoning; in USDA terms, it's a non-intact meat product. You can choose from several different types of meat grinders. (For more information on grinders, refer to Chapter 1.)

Several factors come into play when grinding sausage, and you will need to take them into consideration to ensure the best results.

>> **Sanitation:** You want to make sure you don't make yourself or anyone else sick. To reduce the chances of this happening, before you get started, you should thoroughly wash your hands, and clean your work area and all equipment that you will be using to grind your sausage. Chapter 1 contains a great deal of information on proper hygiene and sanitation; take a gander if you haven't already!

>> **Temperature control:** Your meat mixture needs to be kept as cold as possible (without freezing). This is to control the growth of bacteria and to ensure that the fats in your meat mixture don't begin to smear. Smearing won't hurt you, but the meat doesn't look as pretty at the end of the process.

TIP

To drop the temperature of the meat, try putting it into the freezer for 10 to 20 minutes before grinding.

>> **Proper seasoning:** Nothing is worse than swollen hands and fingers after a night of eating salty foods — or maybe even worse, singing Johnny Cash the morning after a run-in with an overly spicy meal!

>> **Protein-to-fat ratio:** I love full-flavored food just as much as the next guy, but nobody wants a sausage that is 50 percent fat — even folks on the keto diet.

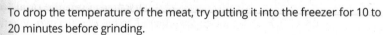

Meat preparations

Before you can grind your meat, you need to prepare it. You will first need to determine your protein-to-fat ratio. Typical sausages are 70 percent lean, meaning that the total weight of the sausage is 70 percent protein and 30 percent fat. You can have a sausage that is 60 percent lean, but it will definitely be a fatty sausage. I suggest that you start by making your sausages 80 percent lean for a couple of reasons:

» **Leaner sausages render less fat when cooked.** *Rendering* is a technical way to say "melting." When you render fat, you lose mass. Naturally, a sausage that renders less fat will be more substantial in size when it is cooked.

» **Fat provides flavor and retains flavorings.** Fat also provides that juicy texture — that is, when you cook your sausage right.

To calculate an 80-percent-protein to 20-percent-fat ratio, you will multiply the total weight of your batch by the percent of protein and fat, respectively. For example,

10 lbs. of sausage at a ratio of 80/20 =

(.8 * 10 lbs.) = 8 lbs. protein

(.2 * 10 lbs.) = 2 lbs. fat

Once you have calculated the amount of protein and fat that you want, you need to portion them out separately to ensure you have the correct ratio. For ultimate precision, you will need to trim fat from your protein using a knife. However, many recipes will allow you to substitute pork belly for fat because of its high fat content.

Before you grind, you will need to break down your protein and fat into pieces small enough to fit into your grinder. This is a good time to separate the fat from the protein for your recipe. Figure 5-1 illustrates a reasonably sized chunk of meat in relation to the size of the grinder hopper opening.

Grinding is a very intense mechanical process that generates a lot of heat through friction. As a result, it's important to break your meat down into smaller pieces to reduce the amount each piece is worked by the grinder; this will reduce the amount of heat-producing friction during grinding.

FIGURE 5-1:
Meat sized for the
grinder hopper
opening.

Spices are the spice of life

When measuring spices and ingredients for your sausage recipes, you can opt to use volume measures (cups, tablespoons, teaspoons, and so on) or weights (pounds, ounces, and grams). The most precise recipes will rely on weights that are relative to the weight of your protein and fat. Volumes can be deceiving because of the size and shape of the ingredients. For example, kosher salt is less dense than sea salt, and so a tablespoon of kosher salt is much less salt than a tablespoon of sea salt. However, 10 grams of kosher salt is the same amount of salt as 10 grams of sea salt. For precision, all of the measures in this book are in grams, and calculated by percent of protein and fat mass.

Using recipes that rely on weight measures will make it easier to modify those recipes by increasing or decreasing the weights.

There are several schools of thought on when ingredients should be added to your protein and fat. I suggest that you add dry ingredients prior to grinding. This is because as the mixture is ground, it is also mixing, and this helps ensure that you have a more even distribution of ingredients throughout the meat mixture. For this reason, all ingredients will need to be measured before you can start grinding. Figure 5-2 shows meat and ingredients prior to grinding.

Wet ingredients are always incorporated after the meat mixture is ground. Water, vinegar, wine, fruit juices, and so on will blend into a ground meat mixture and not wash off.

FIGURE 5-2:
Meat and
ingredients prior
to mixing and
grinding.

Photo by David Pluimer

Time to grind

You're going to get tired of hearing this, but I'll say it anyway: Temperature control is of the utmost importance! Meat grinding produces heat through friction, but cold meat is safer and less likely to smear when grinding. An additional step that you can take to avoid temperature increases is to place your grinder hopper (with the worm, knife, plate, and locking ring installed) in the freezer prior to grinding. After the assembly is freezing cold, you can connect it to the grinder once you're ready to start grinding.

The size of the holes in the plate on your grinder will determine how coarse or fine your grind is. Figure 5-3 shows a comparison of different plates. If you intend to have a fine grind, you will want to start with a plate that has larger-diameter holes and then re-grind with a plate that has smaller-diameter holes. This approach will get you a fine grind with less friction along the way. Your recipe will dictate the grind and size of plates that you use.

WARNING

A word about safety: Grinders are powerful machines that can cause severe bodily harm when not used appropriately. Your electric grinder should have a meat tray, a guard of some sort around and over the hopper opening (see Figure 5-4a), and a stuffing tool (see Figure 5-4b). Never stick your hand or fingers into the hopper. It is very easy for your fingers to get drawn down inside, and finger sausage is gross and very painful to make. Make sure you never use your fingers to stuff a meat mixture into the grinder. Instead, use the stuffing tool, and rely on the guard for extra safety.

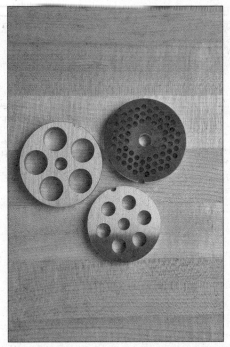

FIGURE 5-3:
Plates with holes
of different
diameters.

Photo by David Pluimer

FIGURE 5-4:
Grinder hopper
guard and
stuffing tool.

Photo by David Pluimer

Just prior to grinding, combine your dry ingredients with your meat and fat mixture. Thoroughly mix them until all the dry ingredients are adhering to the mixture. Then power on your grinder and start carefully running the mixture through the grinder. Once your mixture has been ground, hand-mix it for a minute or two. Proteins contain a compound called *myocin* that will help bind your ground mixture. Mixing by hand for a couple of minutes will help activate it. Once you are finished mixing by hand, cover the mixture with some plastic wrap and refrigerate it overnight.

Emulsified Sausages

Emulsified sausages are known for their extremely tender and moist texture. If you've ever had a hot dog, you've had an emulsified sausage. Other examples of emulsified sausage include frankfurters, bologna, mortadella, weisswurst, and liverwurst. The principles of making an emulsified sausage are very similar to those for ground sausages, but an extra step or two is involved.

Emulsified sausages are made by finely chopping and blending a ground meat mixture with spices, wet ingredients, and ice to form a paste. The paste is then stuffed into a casing and fully cooked by either poaching in water or hot smoking. These sausages are called *emulsified* because you have to create a fully incorporated mixture of meat and liquid. To do this, you will require one additional piece of equipment known as a *bowl chopper* or *buffalo chopper*. The home version of this is called a *food processor*, an example of which is pictured in Figure 5-5.

FIGURE 5-5: Food processor.

Photo by David Pluimer

The steps to making an emulsified sausage are similar to those for a ground sausage, with the additional step of finely mincing, almost pureeing, the ground meat mixture. Some emulsified sausages also require a cooking step.

1. **Portion and prepare your meat mixture.**
2. **Portion the dry and wet ingredients.**
3. **Chill the grinder parts.**
4. **Grind the meat mixture.**
5. **Add the meat mixture, spices, and liquid ingredients to a food processor, and puree.**
6. **Chill the meat mixture overnight.**

A Word about Casings

In the wild world of sausage, you have two options for finishing your product. You can either leave your sausage mixture loose (an option really reserved for ground, not emulsified sausages), or you can stuff your sausage into a casing. Casings are the tubes that form and hold your sausage mixture together. They come in a lot of different shapes, sizes, and materials, and they all have different applications. Following is a list of the major categories of casings:

>> **Natural casing.** This sounds as awesome as you may be imagining. Natural (gut) casing is derived from the intestines of pigs, sheep, or cows. Each species has attributes that make them desirable for different applications.

- **Hog casing.** These casings are great for fresh and smoked sausages because of their durability and size. They are somewhat durable and not as prone to tearing as sheep or collagen casings. They aren't too thick, which means they aren't tough to chew through. Hog casings range in size from 28 to 42 mm in diameter.

- **Sheep casing.** Smaller critters have smaller guts, and sheep are no exception. Casings made from the intestines of sheep are smaller in diameter, and much more fragile than hog casings. They are an ideal size for breakfast sausage links. Sheep casings can range in size from 19 to 26 mm in diameter.

- **Beef middles casing.** Beef middles are the thick sections of a cow's intestine. They are extremely durable and are generally used for making salamis. Beef middles aren't edible and are usually peeled off prior to eating. Beef middles range in size from 2 to 2.5 inches in diameter.

- **Beef bung casing.** Beef bung is the appendix of a cow. Large-format salamis are cased in beef bungs, and are sealed off on one side. These casings are extremely durable but not all that edible. Beef bungs range in size from 4.5 to 5 inches in diameter and are approximately 18 inches in length.

  Figure 5-6 shows several different types of casings next to each other to give you context for the differences.

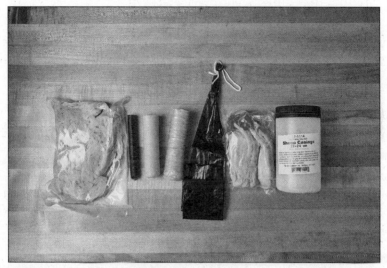

FIGURE 5-6:
Hog, sheep, and beef casings.

>> **Fibrous casing.** Cellulose-based casings are strengthened with natural plant fibers. This gives these casings extra strength to ensure very tight fills. Fibrous casings breathe, which means that when you smoke them, the smoke penetrates the meat to impart a smoky flavor. Fibrous casings are not edible. Fully cooked summer sausage typically uses these casings. Figure 5-7 shows an example of a fibrous casing.

>> **Cellulose casing.** Cellulose casings are similar to fibrous casings, but they lack the additional plant fibers that give fibrous casings the additional strength needed for larger-diameter sausages. Cellulose casings are generally used for hot dogs and frankfurters. They are peeled off after cooking, which makes the sausages "case-less."

» **Collagen casing.** Collagen casings are derived from animals, primarily cows. The materials are extracted from the hide of a cow, as well as its bones and tendons. A collagen casing is edible and permeable. This style of casing is growing in popularity because it is easier to use than gut (natural) casings. At Old Major Market, we use collagen casings for all of our breakfast links. Figure 5-8 shows a collagen casing.

FIGURE 5-7:
Fibrous casing prior to stuffing.

Photo by David Pluimer

Where to buy sausage casings

There are several options for buying sausage casings on (you probably know what I'm going to say) the internet! If you have a local butcher, they may have some sausage casings that you can buy, but your best bet is to purchase your casings online. In Chapter 1, I list several options for purchasing equipment, but these are also great resources for finding sausage casings.

TIP

If you don't want to flip back, here's a quick list in my order of preference:

www.SausageMaker.com

www.butcher-packer.com

www.waltonsinc.com

FIGURE 5-8:
Collagen casing.

Photo by David Pluimer

Fibrous, cellulose, collagen, and even beef middles and bungs don't come with many, potentially confusing, options. You can shop based on the size, color, and quantity of the casings. Sheep and hog casings tend to have quite a few options that can affect both the cost of your sausage and the quality of the end result. Here are some things to consider when shopping for sheep and hog casings:

>> **Pre-tubed or not.** In order to stuff a sausage casing, you will need to place the casing over the horn of your stuffer. A tubed casing is simply a casing that has a hollow plastic sheath running through it. This makes it very quick and easy to get an entire casing on the horn of your stuffer. If the casing is not pre-tubed, the job of putting the casing on the horn will take a little bit longer.

>> **Whiskers.** "Whiskers" are the capillaries that provide blood flow to the intestines. When the intestines are removed with a knife, these capillaries may not be completely removed. What is left over looks like a whisker. Whiskers generally disappear during cooking, but if you don't like their appearance, you can purchase a whisker-free product that is "shaved." Another option is to purchase an inverted casing so that the whiskers are on the inside and not visible.

>> **Packing.** Natural casings can be packed in several different ways. The two most common types of packages that you will run into are listed here:

- **Dry salted.** These casings are sold in bags or plastic tubs and are packed in a large quantity of dry salt. They are usually cheaper than casings packed in salt water, but generally require extra time to prep for use.

- **Wet brine.** These casings are packed in bags or buckets of extremely salty water. They are a little more expensive than dry-salted casings, but they require less prep time prior to usage.

Care and prep of casings

Natural casings, regardless of how they are packed, should be kept refrigerated. This will ensure their maximum lifespan. All other casings should be kept sealed and in a bag, and stored in a dark, cool, dry place. Collagen casings are extremely susceptible to changes in humidity. They are usually packaged in sealed plastic or Mylar bags with desiccant packets to ensure there is little to no humidity in the packaging.

When you start gearing up to stuff sausages, some prep work will be involved to get your casings ready to use. Cellulose and collagen casings do not need to be soaked in water prior to use; in fact, soaking collagen casings in water will ruin them. Fibrous casings will benefit from a brief soak in warm water. Natural (gut) casings, however, require the most TLC when being prepped for use. For dry-salted casings, follow these steps to get them ready:

1. **The packaging for your casings should tell you approximately how many pounds you can stuff with the casings contained within. Be sure to hydrate the appropriate amount of casings for the job at hand!**

TIP

Make sure you hydrate more casings than you need. You will probably not fill them perfectly, and you will likely break several as you learn how to stuff sausages. There is nothing worse than running out of casings in the middle of stuffing sausages!

2. **Rinse salt from the casings with fresh water. I like to put the casings in a bowl and vigorously agitate the casings in the water with my fingers.**

3. **Soften the casings by soaking them in fresh water at room temperature (approximately 70 degrees Fahrenheit) for 45 minutes to one hour. Gently massage the casings to ensure there are no dry spots.**

TIP

Soaking overnight in the refrigerator is acceptable as well. Although this *can* make your casings slightly more fragile, I have never had a problem.

4. **Flush the casings by running fresh water into them and allowing it to run through them.**

5. **Just prior to stuffing, transfer the casings into a clean bucket of 80-degree-Fahrenheit fresh water. This will loosen them up further and allow them to slide on and off the stuffing horn with greater ease.**

If you have casings that are packed in a wet brine, you can get away with just performing Steps 1 and 4.

When you are finished stuffing, if there are any casings left, save them by packing them in a bag or airtight container, and cover them with an excessive amount of salt. The salt will make the environment toxic to bacteria and will ensure safe storage in the fridge until you are ready to make sausage again!

Stuffing and Linking Sausage

True to their name, sausage stuffers are specialized pieces of equipment intended primarily for stuffing sausages. They come in all sizes and shapes. When I launched into the sausage-making business, I started off with an 11-pound-capacity manual stuffer. We upgraded to a No. 30–capacity stuffer and used it for a couple of years. The last year we used it exclusively, we made over 3000 lbs of sausage with it. My left shoulder looked RIPPED! Now we've upgraded to an automated machine that helps us stuff and link upwards of 500 pounds of sausage in an hour!

Figure 5-9 is a picture of our three stuffers. With each upgrade we were able to achieve large increases in productivity. Our Lucky Linker, however, has been a total game changer! In Chapter 1 I cover stuffers, so if you want a quick primer, check it out.

If you are using natural casings, before you can stuff a sausage, you need to make sure your casings are hydrated and flushed.

Your sausage stuffer is going to require a little prep work before you can stuff your first foot of sausage. If you have a friend to help, this would be a great time for them to join in the process!

1. **Sanitation:** By now this should sound like a broken record, but make sure that before you get started, you have thoroughly washed your hands, and also cleaned your work area and all stuffing equipment. (You can find a great deal of information on proper hygiene and sanitation in Chapter 1.) There are many places where junk can hide in your stuffer. Check all of the seals, welds, threads, and so on, and make sure there is nothing hiding.

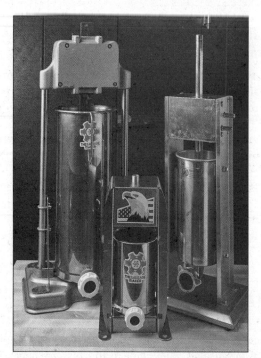

Photo by David Pluimer

2. **Temperature control:** When working with potentially hazardous food, this will always be a concern. Make sure your sausage mixture is left in the fridge as long as possible. You can even leave it in the freezer to drop the temperature even more prior to stuffing. You can also keep the stuffer cylinder in the freezer to cool its temperature down prior to filling the stuffer.

3. **Loading the stuffer:** When stuffing sausage, you want to make sure you minimize the air bubbles that get into your sausage. Your first line of defense against getting air bubbles in your links is to make sure the stuffer is loaded properly. As you are adding ground meat into the cylinder, remember to smash it down with your hand. Keep working the grind in this manner until you've loaded all of it (or the cylinder is full).

4. **Setting up the stuffer:** Once your cylinder is filled with grind, place the cylinder into the stuffer assembly and attach the horn to the cylinder with the locking ring. You will want to use the horn that is closest in size to the diameter of the casing you are using. Figure 5-10 shows a horn being attached to a stuffer.

5. **Clamping down the stuffer:** When you start cranking the stuffer plunger down, you will find that the stuffer has a tendency to slide all over the place. If you don't have a partner to help you by holding the stuffer in place, consider getting some clamps to secure the stuffer to your work surface, similar to the setup shown in Figure 5-11.

Photo by David Pluimer

FIGURE 5-10:
Stuffer assembly.

Phot by David Pluimer

FIGURE 5-11:
Clamp it down.

Stuffing sausage

If you've ever watched a seasoned sausage maker stuff sausages, it may have looked like a breeze. But what you probably didn't notice were the many different points of finesse that they learned from years of making sausages. The speed of the stuffer is controlled by the speed with which you crank the plunger down. The fill level of the sausage casing is controlled by the amount of tension applied to the casing on the horn. The greater the tension, the slower the casing will slip off the horn. Conversely, the lower the tension, the *faster* the casing will slip off the horn. If you are watching a pro, they are coordinating all of this on the fly by managing speed with one hand and applying varying degrees of tension with the other hand.

REMEMBER

Stuffing sausages is a careful balancing act between speed of fill and tension on the sausage casing as it comes off the horn. Casings can only handle so much pressure before they break. The more you do you this activity, the more you will develop a feel for the process and even be able to sense when your casing has been filled to its absolute limit just before it pops. It's something at which you cannot be awesome until you've logged some hours. You need a little muscle memory, so give yourself a grace period when you get started.

The art to stuffing a sausage really lies in the way you handle the casing on the horn. This may sound ridiculous, but you have to get familiar with your casing. You need to get a sense of how hydrated it is, and how much wider it is than your horn. If your casing is properly hydrated and moves freely up and down the horn, then the application of tension to the casing as it is filled with grind will be controlled almost completely by you. If the casing is not as hydrated as it could be, or is a little tight on the horn, then the casing will drag across the horn. The further back you push the casing on the horn toward the base, the more drag will be created on the casing because of the distance it has to travel to get to the end of the horn.

To begin stuffing, you first need to load a casing onto the horn. Figure 5-12 illustrates how to do this.

Once the casing is on the horn, you can either choose to slide a little off the end of the horn and tie a knot, or leave it without a knot. The knot eliminates the problem of grind squirting out the end when you get started. However, you can simply pinch the end of the casing between your fingers to keep that from happening. If you are stuffing an emulsified sausage, then tying the end off will be imperative because the sausage mixture will be quite loose and will run out the end.

TIP

If you opt for tying the end of the casing, prior to doing so you should crank the stuffer down to get sausage to the end of the horn. If you don't, you will push nothing but air into your sealed casing and you will need to poke holes to purge the air from the casing. This is another reason for not tying the end.

With the casing on the horn, begin slowly cranking the plunger down. Position your other hand on the horn as illustrated in Figure 5-13. Be sure to pay attention to how easily the plunger is pushing the grind down into the horn. You will want to get acclimated to the speed at which it can and will flow into and out of the horn. Let the casing start to fill, and use your right hand to apply tension by gently pressing the casing against the horn. This will make it harder for the pressure of the sausage coming out of the horn to drag the casing along and off the horn.

Photos by David Pluimer

FIGURE 5-12:
Progression of
loading a casing
onto the stuffer
horn.

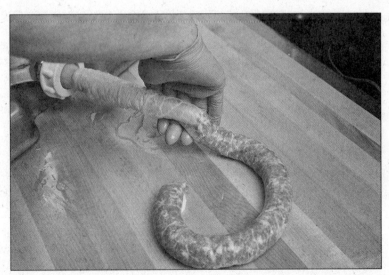

FIGURE 5-13:
Hand positioning
on the stuffer.

Photo by David Pluimer

I am right-hand dominant. When I stuff sausage with a manual stuffer, I crank with my left hand and I use my right hand to manage the horn. I refer to my right hand as the "brake" because I use it to slow down the speed at which the casing slips off the horn.

WARNING

No matter how hard you try to eliminate air bubbles when loading the cylinder, you will have air bubbles. When the air hits the casing, it will cause the casing to puff up like a balloon. This air pressure can cause the casing to break. Air bubbles will also cause you to have a poor fill in the casing. Periodically, if you get air bubbles in the casing while it's on the horn, you should use a sausage pricker (refer to Chapter 1 if you are unfamiliar with this tool) to poke a couple of holes in the casing so the air can escape.

Slowly crank the plunger down and keep filling until you run out of casing. If you run into issues like the casing slipping off, resulting in loose or poor fills, just stop cranking, and then crank in the opposite direction to relieve the pressure inside the cylinder (which will stop the flow of grind out of the horn). Then slide the casing back onto the horn and start again.

REMEMBER

The more sausage you make, the better you will get. Just take your time, there is no rush.

If you are planning to link your sausage, make sure your fill is tight but not so tight that there is no margin for twisting the casings to make links.

TIP

As your sausage casing comes off the end of the horn, periodically stop to coil your sausage rope neatly on the work surface. This will ensure that nothing slips off the counter onto the floor. It is pretty difficult to catch 15 feet of sausage as it slides off the countertop. Before you throw your ring of sausage into a tub and put it into the fridge until it's time to link, you will want to work out any air bubbles that may be in the sausage. Using your sausage pricker, prick your sausage rope from end to end. As you link, this will give the air a place to go and will allow the grind to compress as you twist links.

Linking sausage

If you're ready to link, that means you've stuffed your sausage and hopefully you've got a tub filled with ropes of sausage! Linking sausage is a little more straightforward than stuffing, but there is still quite a bit of finesse involved. If you've filled your casings perfectly, then the task of linking will be pretty straightforward. Probably a little more realistically, this is going to be a process of cleaning up your stuffing job.

Have you ever seen a balloon animal being made? A long, skinny balloon is filled with air and then twisted in all different directions until it is shaped into an animal form or some other object. Have you ever noticed how the balloon is handled by the person making the balloon animal? They tend to use their whole hand to grip, twist, and fashion the balloon. The reason for this is that it spreads pressure out over a greater surface area and reduces the chances that the balloon will pop. This is the same sort of mindset that you need to have when linking sausage.

Your sausage rope is under pressure. As you twist the rope to form links, you are reducing the available space inside the casing, which further compresses the contents. With each twist of the casing, you are increasing pressure. So you need to approach linking with the mindset of "how do I not blow up my balloon?" Just like stuffing, the more you link, the more sense you will get for the process (this is called muscle memory), so you just need to get started.

1. **To begin, empty your rope onto the countertop and form it into a coil.**

2. **Pick up the end of the rope and pinch the outside with one hand. Then, with the other hand, using the space in between your index finger and your thumb, gently compress the link to create a space that you can pinch. Figure 5-14 illustrates this technique.**

3. **Gently spin the sausage link forward (clockwise). Give it a solid five or six spins.**

4. **Repeat Steps 1 and 2. When you are ready to spin your link, you want to spin in the opposite direction of the last link. In this case, you will spin backwards (counter-clockwise).**

REMEMBER

Twisting links compresses your sausage fill. If your links are not rigid after twisting, try spinning them a few more times to compress them further. You want your links to be tightly filled but not bursting.

If you find that your sausage ropes have sections that are so full that they will likely burst, then try spreading the fill out through the casing by gently pushing the fill down the rope to more evenly distribute it. You want to use your whole hand to distribute the pressure out over as much surface area as possible. Grip the sausage rope with your whole hand and gently work the fill down the rope to distribute the fill. You want to start by creating room in a part of the rope that has a light fill and then slowly work your way back toward the section of sausage rope that is under a great deal of pressure.

FIGURE 5-14:
Steps to distribute fill within a sausage rope.

Photos by David Pluimer

Now that your sausage is linked, find a place to hang the ropes of sausage links in your refrigerator so they can "bloom." This is a process of drying the casings and letting the flavors permeate further through the grind. If you can't hang them, leave them in your tub, uncovered, in the fridge overnight before cooking them. You'll appreciate the final product more.

Chapter **6**

Getting Fresh with Sausages

You're Abe Froman, the Sausage King of Chicago?
— MAÎTRE D' AT CHEZ QUIS, *FERRIS BUELLER'S DAY OFF*

S ausage making can be as plain or as extravagant as you want it to be. I think that's one of the things I love about it. You can make sausages with any protein you want. You can season and flavor it with anything you like. Sausages are little handheld, edible time capsules telling a story of people and place. You can make the same sausage a seemingly endless number of ways to suit your preferences.

I selected the recipes for this chapter to give you a wide variety of options: proteins, ingredients, and textures. Try out a few of these sausages to gain some experience behind the stuffer. Before you stuff your sausages, take a little bit of the grind mixture and cook it in a pan. Taste it and make sure you are satisfied. If you think the mixture needs more of something to suit your tastes, then be scientific about it and weigh the additions; then document them so that you can update the recipe to reflect your preferences.

TIP

If you haven't read Chapter 5, I would suggest you push pause and give it a good, solid read-through. It will give you a good primer on how the sausage is made. But if you simply can't do that and instead need to learn by doing, then at least bookmark it so you can quickly reference it if you run into problems.

Breakfast Sausage

PRE-PREP TIME: 15 MINUTES	PREP TIME: 1 HOUR + 1 DAY	CURING TIME: 7 DAYS	YIELD: 4 LBS.

INGREDIENTS

40 grams (1.75%) sea salt

1 gram (.045%) dried parsley

2 grams (.09%) dried rubbed sage

5 grams (.22%) coarse ground black pepper

1 gram (.045%) dried thyme

1 gram (.045%) crushed red pepper flakes

2 grams (.09%) ground coriander

4 lbs. boneless pork shoulder

1 lb. pork fat (or fresh pork belly)

Hydrated and flushed lamb casings

1 Combine the dry ingredients in a mixing bowl, and set aside.

2 Cut the pork shoulder and pork fat / pork belly into pieces small enough to fit into your grinder.

3 In a large mixing bowl or food-safe plastic tub, combine the dry ingredients with the protein and fat. Mix thoroughly.

4 Place the seasoned meat mixture into the freezer for an hour.

5 Place the grinder head, #3/8-inch plate, and #3/16-inch plate into the freezer for an hour.

6 Assemble the grinder head with the #3/8-inch plate.

7 Grind the seasoned meat mixture into a large bowl.

8 Change out the #3/8-inch grinder plate for the #3/16-inch grinder plate.

9 Grind the mixture for a second time into a large bowl.

10 Mix the ground sausage with your hands for 2 minutes.

11 Press the mixture into the bowl bottom and cover the mixture with plastic wrap. Get all of the air out.

12 Refrigerate the mixture overnight.

13 Stuff the sausage into lamb casings for links, or leave it uncased for bulk sausage.

TIP: Make sure your casings have been hydrated overnight prior to stuffing.

REMEMBER: Chill the grinder head and stuffing cylinder prior to using them to help control the temperature.

Pork Bratwurst

PRE-PREP TIME: 15 MINUTES	PREP TIME: 1 HOUR + 1 DAY	YIELD: 5 LBS.

INGREDIENTS

40 grams (1.75%) sea salt

13 grams (.58%) granulated sugar

4 grams (.18%) ground nutmeg

1 gram (.04%) ground coriander

1 gram (.04%) celery seed

2 grams (.09%) ground ginger

5 grams (.22%) coarse ground black pepper

4 lbs. boneless pork shoulder

1 lb. pork fat (or fresh pork belly)

Hydrated and flushed hog casings (29–32 mm)

1 Combine the dry ingredients in a mixing bowl, and set aside.

2 Cut the pork shoulder and pork fat / pork belly into pieces small enough to fit into your grinder.

3 In a large mixing bowl or food-safe plastic tub, combine the dry ingredients with the protein and fat. Mix thoroughly.

4 Place the seasoned meat mixture into the freezer for an hour.

5 Place the grinder head and #3/16-inch plate into the freezer for an hour.

6 Assemble the grinder head with the #3/16-inch plate.

7 Grind the seasoned meat mixture into a large bowl.

8 Mix the ground sausage with your hands for 2 minutes.

9 Press the mixture into the bowl bottom and cover the mixture with plastic wrap. Get all of the air out.

10 Refrigerate the mixture overnight.

11 Stuff the sausage into hog casings; twist the links.

TIP: Make sure your casings have been hydrated overnight prior to stuffing.

REMEMBER: Chill the grinder head and stuffing cylinder prior to using them to help control the temperature.

Venison Hunter's Sausage

PRE-PREP TIME: 15 MINUTES	PREP TIME: 1 HOUR + 1 DAY	YIELD: 5 LBS.

INGREDIENTS

10 grams (1.75%) sea salt

2 grams (.1%) ground nutmeg

5 grams (.2%) ground allspice

3 grams (.15%) ground clove

11 grams (.5%) coarsely ground coriander

11 grams (.5%) coarse ground black pepper

4 lbs. boneless venison trim

1 lb. fresh pork belly

Hydrated and flushed hog casings (29–32 mm)

1 Combine the dry ingredients in a mixing bowl, and set aside

2 Cut the venison and pork belly into pieces small enough to fit into your grinder.

3 In a large mixing bowl or food-safe plastic tub, combine the dry ingredients with the protein and fat. Mix thoroughly.

4 Place the seasoned meat mixture into the freezer for an hour.

5 Place the grinder head and #3/16-inch plate into the freezer for an hour.

6 Assemble the grinder head with the #3/16-inch plate.

7 Grind the seasoned meat mixture into a large bowl.

8 Mix the ground sausage with your hands for 2 minutes.

9 Press the mixture into the bowl bottom and cover the mixture with plastic wrap. Get all of the air out.

10 Refrigerate the mixture overnight.

11 Stuff the sausage into hog casings; twist the links.

TIP: Make sure your casings have been hydrated overnight prior to stuffing.

REMEMBER: Chill the grinder head and stuffing cylinder prior to using them to help control the temperature.

Island Chicken Sausage

PRE-PREP TIME: 15 MINUTES	PREP TIME: 1 HOUR + 1 DAY	YIELD: 5 LBS.

INGREDIENTS

40 grams (1.75%) sea salt

9 grams (.4%) granulated sugar

4 grams (.18%) garlic powder

3 grams (.13%) onion powder

6 grams (.26%) cayenne powder

1 gram (.04%) ground allspice

1 gram (.04%) ground nutmeg

1 gram (.04%) dried thyme

2 grams (.09%) dried parsley

2 grams (.09%) ground cinnamon

11 grams (.49%) coarse ground black pepper

2 grams (.09%) crushed red pepper flake

5 lbs. boneless, skinless chicken thighs

Hydrated and flushed hog casings (29–32 mm)

1 Combine the dry ingredients in a mixing bowl, and set aside.

2 Cut the boneless, skinless chicken thighs into pieces small enough to fit into your grinder.

3 In a large mixing bowl or food-safe plastic tub, combine the dry ingredients with the protein. Mix thoroughly.

4 Place the seasoned meat mixture into the freezer for an hour.

5 Place the grinder head and #3/16-inch plate into the freezer for an hour.

6 Assemble the grinder head with the #3/16-inch plate.

7 Grind the seasoned meat mixture into a large bowl.

8 Mix the ground sausage with your hands for 2 minutes.

9 Press the mixture into the bowl bottom and cover the mixture with plastic wrap. Get all of the air out.

10 Refrigerate the mixture overnight.

11 Stuff the sausage into hog casings; twist the links.

TIP: Make sure your casings have been hydrated overnight prior to stuffing.

REMEMBER: Chill the grinder head and stuffing cylinder prior to using them to help control the temperature.

TIP: For slightly more fat in the mixture, use boneless, skin-on chicken thighs.

Turkey Cranberry Sausage

PRE-PREP TIME: 15 MINUTES	PREP TIME: 1 HOUR + 1 DAY	YIELD: 5 LBS.

INGREDIENTS

40 grams (1.75%) sea salt

10 grams (.44%) fresh sage

5 grams (.22%) coarse ground black pepper

1 gram (.04%) dried thyme

3 grams (.13%) coarse ground coriander

70 grams (3%) dried cranberries

5 lbs. boneless, skinless turkey thighs

Hydrated and flushed hog casings (29–32 mm)

1 Combine the dry and fresh ingredients in a mixing bowl, and set aside.

2 Cut the boneless, skinless turkey thighs into pieces small enough to fit into your grinder.

3 In a large mixing bowl or food-safe plastic tub, combine the dry ingredients with the protein. Mix thoroughly.

4 Place the seasoned meat mixture into the freezer for an hour.

5 Place the grinder head and #3/16-inch plate into the freezer for an hour.

6 Assemble the grinder head with the #3/16-inch plate.

7 Grind the seasoned meat mixture into a large bowl.

8 Mix the ground sausage with your hands for 2 minutes.

9 Press the mixture into the bowl bottom and cover the mixture with plastic wrap. Get all of the air out.

10 Refrigerate the mixture overnight.

11 Stuff the sausage into hog casings; twist the links.

TIP: Make sure your casings have been hydrated overnight prior to stuffing.

REMEMBER: Chill the grinder head and stuffing cylinder prior to using them to help control the temperature.

TIP: For slightly more fat in the mixture, use boneless, skin-on turkey thighs.

Andouille

PRE-PREP TIME: 15 MINUTES	PREP TIME: 5 HOURS + 1 DAY	YIELD: 5 LBS.

INGREDIENTS

40 grams (1.75%) sea salt

6 grams (.25%) pink salt #1

6 grams (.26%) cayenne powder

1 gram (.04%) dried thyme

2 grams (.09%) ground mace

2 grams (.09%) ground clove

1 gram (.04%) ground allspice

138 grams (6%) diced yellow onion

18 grams (.8%) minced fresh garlic

4 lbs. boneless pork shoulder

1 lb. pork fat (or fresh pork belly)

Hydrated and flushed hog casings (29–32 mm)

1 Combine the dry and fresh ingredients in a mixing bowl, and set aside.

2 Cut the pork shoulder and pork fat / pork belly into pieces small enough to fit into your grinder.

3 In a large mixing bowl or food-safe plastic tub, combine the dry ingredients with the protein and fat. Mix thoroughly.

4 Place the seasoned meat mixture into the freezer for an hour.

5 Place the grinder head and #3/16-inch plate into the freezer for an hour.

6 Assemble the grinder head with the #3/16-inch plate.

7 Grind the seasoned meat mixture into a large bowl.

8 Mix the ground sausage with your hands for 2 minutes.

9 Press the mixture into the bowl bottom and cover the mixture with plastic wrap. Get all of the air out.

10 Refrigerate the mixture overnight.

11 Stuff the sausage into hog casings; twist the links.

12 Place the sausages in a smoker and smoke at 180 degrees Fahrenheit until the internal temperature reaches 145 degrees Fahrenheit. Smoke using hickory or pecan wood.

13 Once the internal temperature is reached, rapidly cool the sausages by immersing them in an ice-water bath for 5 minutes. Remove and refrigerate.

TIP: Make sure your casings have been hydrated overnight prior to stuffing.

REMEMBER: Chill the grinder head and stuffing cylinder prior to using them to help control the temperature.

Smoked Pork Sausage

PRE-PREP TIME: 15 MINUTES	PREP TIME: 5 HOURS + 1 DAY	YIELD: 5 LBS.

INGREDIENTS

40 grams (1.75%) sea salt

6 grams (.25%) pink salt #1

5 grams (.25%) ground marjoram

11 grams (.5%) coarse ground black pepper

14 grams (.6%) fresh garlic cloves (pressed using a garlic press)

4 lbs. boneless pork shoulder

1 lb. pork fat (or fresh pork belly)

Hydrated and flushed hog casings (29–32 mm)

1 Combine the dry and fresh ingredients in a mixing bowl, and set aside.

2 Cut the pork shoulder and pork fat / pork belly into pieces small enough to fit into your grinder.

3 In a large mixing bowl or food-safe plastic tub, combine the dry ingredients with the protein and fat. Mix thoroughly.

4 Place the seasoned meat mixture into the freezer for an hour.

5 Place the grinder head and #3/16-inch plate into the freezer for an hour.

6 Assemble the grinder head with the #3/16-inch plate.

7 Grind the seasoned meat mixture into a large bowl.

8 Mix the ground sausage with your hands for 2 minutes.

9 Press the mixture into the bowl bottom and cover the mixture with plastic wrap. Get all of the air out.

10 Refrigerate the mixture overnight.

11 Stuff the sausage into hog casings; twist the links.

12 Place the sausages in a smoker and smoke them at 180 degrees Fahrenheit until the internal temperature reaches 145 degrees Fahrenheit. Smoke using hickory or pecan wood.

13 Once the internal temperature is reached, rapidly cool the sausages by immersing them in an ice-water bath for 5 minutes. Remove and refrigerate.

TIP: Make sure your casings have been hydrated overnight prior to stuffing.

REMEMBER: Chill the grinder head and stuffing cylinder prior to using them to help control the temperature.

Boudin Blanc

PRE-PREP TIME: 15 MINUTES	PREP TIME: 1 HOUR + 2 DAYS	YIELD: 8 LBS.

INGREDIENTS

62 grams (1.75%) sea salt

6 grams (.18%) ground white pepper

8 grams (.22%) finely ground black pepper

2 grams (.06%) ground nutmeg

2 grams (.06%) ground cinnamon

2 grams (.06%) ground cloves

2 grams (.06%) ground caraway seed

64 grams (1.8%) potato starch

420 grams (18.5%) whole milk

420 grams (18.5%) cream

420 grams (18.5%) eggs

1 cup crushed ice

4 lbs. boneless pork shoulder

1 lb. pork fat (or fresh pork belly)

Hydrated and flushed hog casings (29–32 mm)

1 Combine the dry ingredients in a mixing bowl, and set aside.

2 Cut the pork shoulder and pork fat / pork belly into pieces small enough to fit into your grinder.

3 In a large mixing bowl or food-safe plastic tub, combine the dry ingredients with the protein and fat. Mix thoroughly.

4 Place the seasoned meat mixture into the freezer for an hour.

5 Place the grinder head and #3/16-inch plate into the freezer for an hour.

6 Assemble the grinder head with the #3/16-inch plate.

7 Grind the seasoned meat mixture into a large bowl.

8 Mix the ground sausage with your hands for 2 minutes.

9 Press the mixture into the bowl bottom and cover the mixture with plastic wrap. Get all of the air out.

10 Refrigerate the mixture overnight.

11 Remove the meat mixture from the fridge and place it in the freezer for an hour.

12 Combine and thoroughly mix the milk, cream, and eggs, then return the mixture to the fridge to keep it chilled.

13 In your food processor, combine the meat mixture with the milk, cream, and egg mixture. Your food processor may not be large enough, so you will want to do this in batches. Add one-half cup of crushed ice to the food processor to help keep the mixture cold. This is important because you don't want the mixture to warm up. Process the mixture until it is thoroughly blended (emulsified).

(continued)

14 Store your emulsion in a large bowl, cover it with plastic wrap, and refrigerate it overnight.

15 Stuff the sausage into hog casings. Make sure you tie the ends of your hog casings to ensure none of the mixture spills out of the ends. Twist the links.

16 Gently cook (poach) the sausages in a pot of 170-degree-Fahrenheit water until the sausages are 160 degrees Fahrenheit.

17 Remove and immediately chill the sausages in an ice-water bath. Refrigerate.

18 The sausages are fully cooked at this point. To prepare them for eating, warm a pan and melt a pile of butter. Keep the heat at medium to medium-low. Place a couple of sausages in the pan and baste them with butter. Flip the links every 3 to 4 minutes and keep basting until they are a medium-golden color.

TIP: Make sure your casings have been hydrated overnight prior to stuffing.

TIP: Using ice will help keep your mixture nice and cold. Don't skip that step!

TIP: Using an immersion circulator (often and incorrectly called a *sous vide*) is an easy way to poach sausages at a constant temperature.

REMEMBER: Chill the grinder head and stuffing cylinder prior to using them to help control the temperature.

TIP: The ingredient weights are calculated from the combined weight of the protein and wet ingredients.

Hot Dog

PRE-PREP TIME: 15 MINUTES	PREP TIME: 1 HOUR + 2 DAYS	YIELD: 8 LBS.

INGREDIENTS

62 grams (1.75%) sea salt

6 grams (.25%) pink salt #1

9 grams (.4%) ground white pepper

6 grams (.27%) ground mustard seed

1 gram (.05%) garlic powder

1 cup ice water

5 lbs. beef brisket

Hydrated and flushed sheep casings (29–32 mm)

1   Combine the dry ingredients in a mixing bowl, and set aside.

2   Cut the beef brisket into pieces small enough to fit into your grinder.

3   In a large mixing bowl or food-safe plastic tub, combine the dry ingredients with beef brisket. Mix thoroughly.

4   Place the seasoned meat mixture into the freezer for an hour.

5   Place the grinder head and #3/16-inch plate into the freezer for an hour.

6   Assemble the grinder head with the #3/16-inch plate.

7   Grind the seasoned meat mixture into a large bowl.

8   Mix the ground sausage with your hands for 2 minutes.

9   Press the mixture into the bowl bottom and cover the mixture with plastic wrap. Get all of the air out.

10   Refrigerate the mixture overnight.

11   Remove the meat mixture from the fridge and place it in the freezer for an hour.

12   In your food processor, combine the meat mixture with ice water. Your food processor may not be large enough, so you will want to do this in batches. Process the mixture until it is thoroughly blended (emulsified).

13   Store your emulsion in a large bowl, cover it with plastic wrap, and refrigerate it overnight.

14   Stuff the sausage into sheep casings. Make sure you tie the ends of your sheep casings to ensure none of the mixture spills out of the ends. Twist the links.

(continued)

15 Refrigerate the sausages overnight, uncovered.

16 Remove the sausages from the fridge and hang them in your kitchen for 2 to 4 hours prior to smoking them (which will slightly dry the exteriors). This will allow the smoke to adhere better.

17 Smoke the sausages at 180 degrees Fahrenheit until the internal temperature reaches 145 degrees Fahrenheit. Smoke with hickory or pecan wood.

18 Remove and immediately chill the sausages in an ice-water bath. Refrigerate.

TIP: Make sure your casings have been hydrated overnight prior to stuffing.

REMEMBER: Chill the grinder head and stuffing cylinder prior to using them to help control the temperature.

Chapter **7**

You Say Salami, I Say Salame

The end of the pig is the beginning of the sausage.

— ITALIAN PROVERB

As a kid, my favorite lunchmeat was bologna; not the good stuff, but the pre-sliced stuff found in a clear-and-yellow plastic container. You know the kind I'm talking about. My older brother was more of a salami kind of kid. Same brand, same trash. I don't know what it was about the salami, but I just couldn't get into it. Don't get me wrong, I loved a good peperoni; but it wasn't until I got much older that I started really digging salami.

Salamis in the traditional sense are dry-cured sausages that require no refrigeration, and when done right, they can last quite some time. This technique of preservation is unique because it requires a little more science than simply salting and drying a piece of meat. When you grind protein, any bacteria that existed on the outside of the meat are blended with the inside, outside, and all through the grind mixture. When that mixture is then put into a casing, you are creating ideal conditions for the growth of all sorts of bad bugs.

To protect yourself while the sausage is drying and becoming a hard salami, you need to ensure that the sausage is acidified. That is to say, the pH needs to be lowered to a point that the environment is not conducive to bacterial growth.

At a lower pH, the sausage can then dry to a level of water activity low enough to further protect against spoilage through bacterial propagation.

In this chapter you will explore the different techniques available for acidification. Then you will take a deep dive into acidification using starter cultures. You will also learn how to use good mold to protect yourself against bad mold. Combining the information in this chapter about fermentation with the information in Chapter 4 about drying, you will be armed to make the salami recipes in this chapter!

Fermenting Sausage

When you hear the word "fermentation," you may, like most people, think about the kind of fermentation that occurs in beer or wine. If you are a baker, you may think of bubbling sourdough starters. Or if you are a little crunchier, maybe you'll think about pickles, sauerkraut, or other fermented vegetables. I would be willing to wager that most people don't think about fermented meat.

Sour meat might make your stomach feel a little sour, but it's the sour that is responsible for keeping dry-cured sausages safe and allowing them to last for extended periods of time without refrigeration. The presence of an acid in the sausage is what lowers the pH and gives it a sour flavor.

REMEMBER

pH is the quantitative measure of the acidity or basicity of a liquid solution. The lower the pH, the more acidic it is.

There are a number of different types of acids, many of which you wouldn't want to ingest in high quantities. The most common acid used in the production of salami is *lactic acid.* Animal protein contains many natural bacteria that feed off available sugars and produce lactic acid as a by-product. Think about how yeast is used in brewing. As the yeast consumes sugars, it produces carbon dioxide and alcohol. Many years ago, before the advent of modern food science, salamis were acidified using a technique called *back slopping.* Some meat would be allowed to ferment by resting at room temperature. This meat would be added into a fresh sausage mixture, and the newly combined mixture would be chopped, stuffed, and left to ferment before going to dry. This technique has been around for thousands of years, and many purists still use it today. However, today the process of acidifying with live cultures has become more precise through the use of laboratory-derived fermenting starter cultures.

Note: Another option for acidification is the use of chemical acidulants like encapsulated citric acid and lactic acid. These two acids are coated in a mixture of maltodextrin and hydrogenated vegetable oil. The coatings melt off when the meat mixture is heated to over 135 degrees Fahrenheit. Encapsulated acids only work to acidify meats that are heated, so they are not a good option for salamis made without heat treating. For the scope of this book, I will focus solely on lactic acid starter cultures.

Using a lactic acid starter culture

If you've ever made bread that required yeast to rise, then you're halfway to making your own fermented dry-cured salamis. Lactic acid starter cultures come packaged in little Mylar bags and are made by only a handful of producers in the United States. Bactoferm is a widely available brand and is very reliable. Figure 7-1 is an example of a package of lactic acid starter culture.

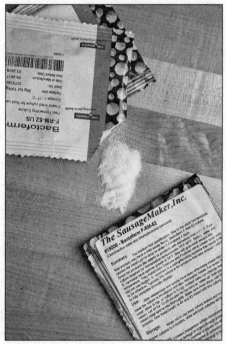

FIGURE 7-1: Bactoferm lactic acid starter culture.

Photo by David Pluimer

There are several different types of fermenting cultures that you can choose from. Each one has its own unique characteristics based on the type of bacteria strains that it contains. When selecting a fermenting culture, you want to pay attention to the temperature at which it needs to be fermented. You also want to pay attention to the amount of time it takes to ferment at that temperature.

There are a handful of places online where you can purchase your starter cultures. Following is a list of reliable online retailers:

```
https://sausagemaker.com

https://butcher-packer.com

https://waltonsinc.com
```

TIP

Fermenting cultures are sensitive to temperature. Store them in the freezer until you are ready to use them.

For the recipes in this book, I advise the use of Bactoferm F-RM-52 starter culture. It is a fast-fermenting culture and can be fermented at temperatures of 70 to 90 degrees Fahrenheit. If the fermentation is done correctly, the pH will drop below 5.0 within 2 to 4 days. Did you pick up on that? Fermenting sausage at 70 degrees Fahrenheit for 2 to 4 days?! When you inoculate your sausage with a lactic acid fermenting culture, you are trying to get the fermenting culture to replicate at a rate faster than the bad bacteria. As the culture is replicating, it is releasing lactic acid, which is making the environment toxic for the bad bacteria. At some point the fermenting culture will either run out of food (sugar) or make the environment too toxic for itself, at which point it, too, will die.

A great deal of research is available on the web about the science of fermenting sausages. I am, however, going to keep it simple and offer a very straightforward set of parameters for you to use with the recipes in this chapter. The process is outlined here:

1. **After your meat has been seasoned, ground, and mixed, in a separate container, combine ½ teaspoon of Bactoferm F-RM-52 with ½ cup of distilled water for every 10 lbs. of meat.**

   Use of distilled water is imperative. If the water contains chlorine, it will kill the culture, rendering it useless.

REMEMBER

2. **Let the mixture sit for 15 to 20 minutes to allow the culture to "wake up."**

3. **Pour the Bactoferm mixture into your meat mixture, and then thoroughly mix it by hand to ensure proper distribution of the culture.**

Letting your sausages ferment

Let's fast forward in the process a little, when your sausages are stuffed, tied, and ready to hang. You will now need to get them into your fermentation chamber. Up until this point, all you've done is add the starter; now you need to get the sausages to warm up so they become a more ideal environment for your starter culture to start taking off. Figure 7-2 shows a dedicated fermentation space.

Smoked belly bacon (see Chapter 4 for this recipe).

Jowl bacon (see Chapter 4 for this recipe).

Rasher back (see Chapter 4 for this recipe).

Mold from the Penicillium family is often found growing on aged cheeses and dry-cured meats, such as these salamis. See Chapter 7 for details.

Pancetta Tesa (Flat Pancetta). You can find this recipe in Chapter 4.

Guanciale (see Chapter 4 for this recipe).

Coppa (see Chapter 4 for this recipe).

Bresaola (see Chapter 4 for this recipe).

Breakfast sausage (see Chapter 6 for this recipe).

Pork bratwurst (see Chapter 6 for this recipe).

Venison hunter's sausage (see Chapter 6 for this recipe).

Island chicken sausage (see Chapter 6 for this recipe).

Turkey cranberry sausage (see Chapter 6 for this recipe).

Andouille (see Chapter 6 for this recipe).

Smoked pork sausage (see Chapter 6 for this recipe).

The Stoneking charcuterie board. See Chapter 8 for more on how to put together a fantastic charcuterie board for entertaining.

Savory tomato jam (recipe in Chapter 8) makes a tasty and attractive addition to your board.

Pickles add nice crunch and acidity. If you want to make your own quick pickle chips, check out the recipe in Chapter 8.

No charcuterie board is complete without cheese. Select a variety of soft and hard cheeses to compliment your meats.

FIGURE 7-2: Professional fermentation chamber.

The Sausage Maker

If you don't have a dedicated fermentation space like the one shown in Figure 7-2, then here are a few alternative ideas to get your sausages fermenting.

>> **Home oven:** Your oven is a nice, sealed, dark space that can be kept relatively humid. You will be relying on ambient temperature, so the temperature in your home will need to be 70 degrees. Hang your sausages in the oven for a few days, leaving the light on; to get the humidity up, you might consider putting a large pan of water in the bottom of the oven.

>> **Plastic food-safe container:** If you don't have a place to hang your sausages, then lay them flat in a food-safe container and place a lid on the top. Leave the container on a counter in a place that isn't drafty so that the temperature inside the container can get up to room temperature and remain there.

>> **Immersion circulator:** If you have an immersion circulator, you could place your sausages into Ziploc bags, press the air out gently, and leave the bags in a water bath for a few days. This will keep your links at a constant temperature, and the humidity will be well controlled because of the relative humidity of your sausages.

>> **Sausage-drying rack:** If you have a sausage-drying rack similar to the one in Figure 7-3, then hang your sausages in a non-drafty area of your home and seal off the rack by wrapping it in plastic wrap. If you can position some water in the makeshift chamber, then this may be helpful in maintaining high relative humidity during the fermentation process.

FIGURE 7-3:
Sausage-drying rack.

The Sausage Maker

With your sausages hanging, all you have to do now is wait. With a little time and a dash of luck, in two to four days you will have salamis that are ready to go into the drying chamber.

Testing the pH of your sausages

Before your salamis can go into the drying chamber, you will want to make sure that your fermentation step was successful. In order to test the pH of the sausages, you will need either a pH meter or pH test strips.

REMEMBER

pH is the measure of how acidic or basic a solution is. It is critical that your salamis reach a pH of 5.3 or lower, so that the pH is acidic enough to stop pathogenic growth.

Starting out with pH test strips

TIP

pH test strips are the most cost-effective way of testing the acidity of your salamis. pH strips have a measurable range from 3.9 to 5.7, and a margin of error of +/-0.2. That means that if you are getting a reading of 5.3, then there is a chance that your salamis could be above the critical limit and not safe. This should be moot if the fermentation step was executed correctly.

To test the pH of your salami using a test strip, follow these steps:

1. Be sure to wash your hands and use food-safe gloves.

2. Remove a salami from the fermentation chamber, and make an incision large enough to insert the pH strip.

3. Change gloves and tear a test strip from your roll of pH test paper, as shown in Figure 7-4.

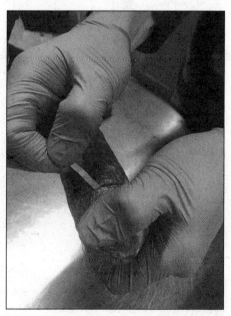

FIGURE 7-4:
Removing pH test paper to test the pH of a salami.

Photo by David Pluimer

4. Insert the test strip into the incision that you made in the salami. Close the salami so that the strip is in complete contact with the grind inside the casing.

After about 5 seconds, the paper should be saturated and the color will have changed.

5. Match the color of the strip with the color guide on the pH strip container to identify the pH of the salami.

Stepping up to a pH meter

pH test paper is a great low-cost way to test your first couple of batches of salami, but if you are planning to make a lot more than that, then you should invest in a pH meter. There are several great products on the market; I suggest that you pick up the Milwaukee Meat pH Meter (shown in Figure 7-5). The device is small, easy to use, and easy to clean. It has a larger pH testing range than the strips, and a margin of error of +/− 0.2.

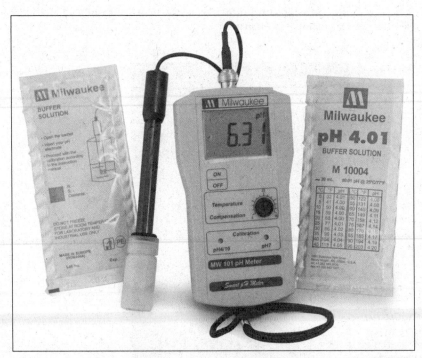

FIGURE 7-5: Milwaukee Meat pH Meter.

The Sausage Maker

To test the pH of your salami, follow these steps:

1. **Be sure to wash your hands and use food-safe gloves.**

2. **Remove a salami from the fermentation chamber.**

3. **Power on the pH meter. Once the display indicates it is ready for use, insert the probe into the salami and wait for the reading to appear.**

If you test your salami after 2 days and the pH hasn't dropped enough yet, then let it keep hanging in the fermentation chamber and test it again in another 48 hours.

WARNING

When fermenting at 70 degrees Fahrenheit, your salami has 110 hours to reach a pH below 5.3. If your salami is at 5.4 or higher, then you should discard the salami and try again.

Ensuring Your Salami Is Secure with a Bubble Knot

Wet casings are slippery little devils, so to ensure that your salami doesn't slip out of a knot and fall onto the floor, you'll want to learn one more knot to get it done right. This knot is referred to as a *bubble knot* and is a surefire way to make sure your salami won't slip out when hanging in the fermentation chamber. Note that in Chapter 4 I explain how to tie a very basic but useful knot. I am going to build on that here in the following steps (see also Figure 7-6):

1. **Draw the string so that it is under the end of your salami.**

   You will want to start your knot over the filled end of the salami so that as you tie your knot, it will slip down a little but may pinch off some of the grind in the salami. This will ensure a tight knot with no air gaps in the end when it is hanging.

2. **Bring the string up on both sides of the salami.**

3. **Cross the string over itself to make an "x."**

4. **Wrap one end over the other three times.**

5. **Carefully pull each end of the string to cinch down the string. Cinch down as hard as you can to ensure a proper seal in the salami.**

6. **Using one end of the string, loop the string around your thumb and finger to create a hitch. Slide the hitch over the end of the casing toward the tie you just made.**

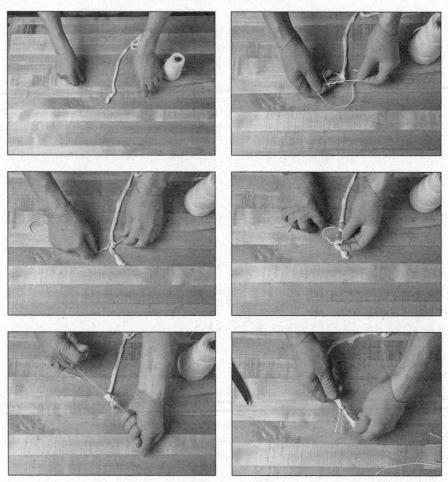

FIGURE 7-6:
Steps to tying a
bubble knot.

Photos by David Pluimer

7. Tighten the hitch down on the casing.

8. One last time, bring the ends of the string together to form an "x."

9. Wrap one end over the other side one time, and pull tight to complete the knot.

Molding the Next Generation of Salami

In Chapter 4, I briefly touch on the good, the bad, and the ugly mold. While there is a lot of suspect mold out there, there is also some good mold: the mold that is used to make blue cheese, and the mold that is used to make antibiotics are two examples. There is even mold that is used to protect cheese and meat while it ages — by the way, that mold is also in the Penicillium family.

In the world of fermented, dry-cured sausage (salami), the use of good mold is a great way to ward off the bad molds of the world. Mold starters are packaged much like fermenting cultures and can be purchased from the same great retailers. For the scope of this book, I use Bactoferm Mold-600 (see Figure 7-7).

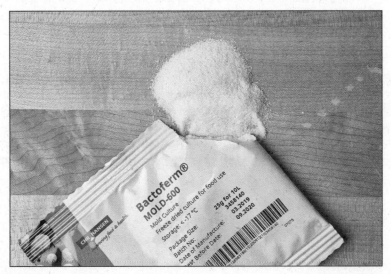

FIGURE 7-7: Bactoferm Mold-600.

Photo by David Pluimer

To put this mold to use, follow these steps:

1. **Mix 5 grams of Bactoferm Mold-600 with 1 liter of distilled water. Allow it to sit for 10 to 15 minutes to "wake up."**

2. **Pour the solution into a spray bottle.**

   If you do not have a spray bottle, you will have to dunk your salamis into the mixture.

3. **Spray the solution on the salamis just before you put them into your fermenting chamber.**

Now all you have to do is wait. As your salamis are fermenting, the mold will also be blooming. You will likely see the mold start to appear just before you put your salamis in the drying chamber.

Drying Your Salami

The salamis described in this book are all smaller-diameter sausages, which means that they will dry in a relatively short amount of time. Because of their size, you want to make sure they don't dry too quickly. Fast drying can inhibit the development of a more complex and desirable flavor profile, and let's be honest: you want to have the tastiest morsels out there, right? Drying too quickly can also cause case hardening, which occurs when the outside is harder than the inside. This will slow the rate at which moisture in the center of the sausages can get out. You can avoid case hardening by vacuum sealing your salami and letting it rest for 30 to 45 days to give the internal moisture a chance to equalize.

TIP

Chapter 4 contains a section on dry curing. For the best and most consistent results, you should invest in a dry-curing chamber. Or, if you are the handy type, you can build your own dry-curing chamber. There is plenty of information available online. In fact, SausageMaker.com has a complete guide to building your own dry-curing chamber out of a refrigerator. Take a look here: http://blog.sausagemaker.com/2015/11/how-to-make-dry-curing-chamber.html

Basic Salami

PREP TIME: 1 HOUR + 1 DAY	FERMENTATION TIME: 2–3 DAYS	DRYING TIME: 3–6 WEEKS

INGREDIENTS

45 grams (2%) sea salt

6 grams (.25%) pink salt #2

10 grams (.45%) cracked black pepper

10 grams (.45%) dextrose

½ teaspoon Bactoferm F-RM-52 starter culture

4 oz. distilled water

4 lbs. boneless pork shoulder

1 lb. pork back fat (or pork belly)

Beef middles, fully hydrated and flushed

1 Combine all of the dry ingredients in a mixing bowl and set aside.

2 Combine the distilled water and Bactoferm starter culture in a dish and set aside.

3 Cut the pork shoulder and pork fat / pork belly into pieces small enough to fit into your grinder.

4 In a large mixing bowl or food-safe plastic tub, combine the dry ingredients with the protein and fat. Mix thoroughly.

5 Place the seasoned meat mixture into the freezer for an hour.

6 Place the grinder head and #3/16" plate into the freezer for an hour.

7 Assemble the grinder head with the #3/16" plate.

8 Grind the seasoned meat mixture into a large bowl.

9 Add the starter culture and water mixture.

10 Mix the ground sausage with your hands for 2 minutes.

11 Press the mixture into the bowl bottom and cover the mixture with plastic wrap. Get all of the air out.

12 Refrigerate the mixture overnight.

13 Cut your beef middles into 8-inch sections. Tie one end of each piece using a square knot (refer to Chapter 4 if you need a refresher).

(continued)

14 Stuff the sausage, fully and tightly, into the beef middles. Once you tie the untied end, you will want the sausage casing to spring back when pressed with your finger.

15 Prick the sausage casing to ensure no air bubbles exist.

16 Spray the sausages with your mold spray (refer to the earlier section, "Molding the Next Generation of Salami," in this chapter).

17 Place the sausages into your fermentation chamber at 70 degrees Fahrenheit and 90-percent humidity. (If you do not have a chamber, refer to the fermentation section in this chapter for alternative options for fermentation.)

18 After 48 hours of fermentation, remove the chub and test it with your pH meter. If the pH is 5.1 or lower, you are ready to dry. If it is not yet at 5.1, allow it to continue fermenting for another 48 hours. Re-test. If it is not below 5.1 at this point, there may have been something wrong with your starter culture. Discard your salamis and start again.

19 Hang your sausages in your drying chamber. Set the temperature to a high threshold of 55 degrees Fahrenheit and a low threshold of 50 degrees Fahrenheit. Set the humidity to 75 percent.

20 After 3 weeks, remove one salami and weigh it. The minimum weight loss should be 30 percent; however, you should target a 40-percent weight loss for a firm salami.

21 If you have reached the proper weight loss, pack your salamis into a vacuum bag and let them rest under vacuum for 30 days to ensure there is no case hardening.

TIP: Using just a little of your grind, stuff a very small sausage, called a *chub*. You will use the chub to test the pH of the salamis.

TIP: Use single-use food-safe gloves for this entire process. Change them often.

WARNING: You are making an uncooked, fermented, ready-to-eat sausage. Hygiene and sanitation are critical to staying safe and managing possible contamination. Clean and sanitize often.

Finocchiona

PREP TIME: 1 HOUR + 1 DAY | FERMENTATION TIME: 2-3 DAYS | DRYING TIME: 3-6 WEEKS

INGREDIENTS

45 grams (2%) sea salt

6 grams (.25%) pink salt #2

6 grams (.25%) coarse ground black pepper

10 grams (.45%) dextrose

12 grams (.53%) toasted and cracked fennel seed

28 grams (1.25%) minced garlic

114 grams (5.03%) Chianti Classico

½ teaspoon Bactoferm F-RM-52 starter culture

4 oz. distilled water

4 lbs. boneless pork shoulder

1 lb. pork back fat (or pork belly)

Beef middles, fully hydrated and flushed

1 Combine all of the dry ingredients in a mixing bowl and set aside.

2 Combine the distilled water and Bactoferm starter culture in a dish and set aside.

3 Cut the pork shoulder and pork fat / pork belly into pieces small enough to fit into your grinder.

4 In a large mixing bowl or food-safe plastic tub, combine the dry ingredients with the protein and fat. Mix thoroughly.

5 Place the seasoned meat mixture into the freezer for an hour.

6 Place the grinder head and #3/16" plate into the freezer for an hour.

7 Assemble the grinder head with the #3/16" plate.

8 Grind the seasoned meat mixture into a large bowl.

9 Add the Chianti Classico.

10 Add the starter culture and water mixture.

11 Mix the ground sausage with your hands for 2 minutes.

12 Press the mixture into the bowl bottom and cover the mixture with plastic wrap. Get all of the air out.

13 Refrigerate the mixture overnight.

14 Cut your beef middles into 8-inch sections. Tie one end of each piece using a square knot (refer to Chapter 4 if you need a refresher).

(continued)

15 Stuff the sausage, fully and tightly, into the beef middles. Once you tie the untied end, you will want the sausage casing to spring back when pressed with your finger.

16 Prick the sausage casing to ensure no air bubbles exist.

17 Spray the sausages with your mold spray (refer to the earlier section, "Molding the Next Generation of Salami," in this chapter).

18 Place the sausages into your fermentation chamber at 70 degrees Fahrenheit and 90-percent humidity. (If you do not have a chamber, refer to the fermentation section in this chapter for alternative options for fermentation.)

19 After 48 hours of fermentation, remove the chub and test it with your pH meter. If the pH is 5.1 or lower, you are ready to dry. If it is not yet at 5.1, allow it to continue fermenting for another 48 hours. Re-test. If it is not below 5.1 at this point, there may have been something wrong with your starter culture. Discard your salamis and start again.

20 Hang your sausages in your drying chamber. Set the temperature to a high threshold of 55 degrees Fahrenheit and a low threshold of 50 degrees Fahrenheit. Set the humidity to 75 percent. Walk away and let your sausages hang for a minimum of 3 weeks.

21 After 3 weeks, remove one salami and weigh it. The minimum weight loss should be 30 percent; however, you should target a 40-percent weight loss for a firm salami.

22 If you have reached the proper weight loss, pack your salamis into a vacuum bag and let them rest under vacuum for 30 days to ensure there is no case hardening.

TIP: Using just a little of your grind, stuff a very small sausage, called a *chub*. You will use the chub to test the pH of the salamis.

TIP: Use single-use food-safe gloves for this entire process. Change them often.

WARNING: You are making an uncooked, fermented, ready-to-eat sausage. Hygiene and sanitation are critical to staying safe and managing possible contamination. Clean and sanitize often.

Picante

PREP TIME: 1 HOUR +
1 DAY

FERMENTATION TIME:
2–3 DAYS

DRYING TIME: 3–6 WEEKS

INGREDIENTS

45 grams (2%) sea salt

6 grams (.25%) pink salt #2

28 grams (1.25%) crushed red pepper flakes

10 grams (.45%) dextrose

28 grams (1.25%) Spanish paprika

14 grams (.62%) cayenne powder

28 grams (1.25%) minced garlic

34 grams (1.5%) cognac

½ teaspoon Bactoferm F-RM-52 starter culture

4 oz. distilled water

4 lbs. boneless pork shoulder

1 lb. pork back fat (or pork belly)

Beef middles, fully hydrated and flushed

1 Combine all of the dry ingredients and garlic in a mixing bowl and set aside.

2 Combine the distilled water and Bactoferm starter culture in a dish and set aside.

3 Cut the pork shoulder and pork fat / pork belly into pieces small enough to fit into your grinder.

4 In a large mixing bowl or food-safe plastic tub, combine the dry ingredients with the protein and fat. Mix thoroughly.

5 Place the seasoned meat mixture into the freezer for an hour.

6 Place the grinder head and #3/16" plate into the freezer for an hour.

7 Assemble the grinder head with the #3/16" plate.

8 Grind the seasoned meat mixture into a large bowl.

9 Add the cognac.

10 Add the starter culture and water mixture.

11 Mix the ground sausage with your hands for 2 minutes.

12 Press the mixture into the bowl bottom and cover the mixture with plastic wrap. Get all of the air out.

13 Refrigerate the mixture overnight.

14 Cut your beef middles into 8-inch sections. Tie one end of each piece using a square knot (refer to Chapter 4 if you need a refresher).

(continued)

15 Stuff the sausage, fully and tightly, into the beef middles. Once you tie the untied end, you will want the sausage casing to spring back when pressed with your finger.

16 Prick the sausage casing to ensure no air bubbles exist.

17 Spray the sausages with your mold spray (refer to the earlier section, "Molding the Next Generation of Salami," in this chapter).

18 Place the sausages into your fermentation chamber at 70 degrees Fahrenheit and 90-percent humidity. (If you do not have a chamber, refer to the fermentation section in this chapter for alternative options for fermentation.)

19 After 48 hours of fermentation, remove the chub and test it with your pH meter. If the pH is 5.1 or lower, you are ready to dry. If it is not yet at 5.1, allow it to continue fermenting for another 48 hours. Re-test. If it is not below 5.1 at this point, there may have been something wrong with your starter culture. Discard your salamis and start again.

20 Hang your sausages in your drying chamber. Set the temperature to a high threshold of 55 degrees Fahrenheit and a low threshold of 50 degrees Fahrenheit. Set the humidity to 75 percent. Walk away and let your sausages hang for a minimum of 3 weeks.

21 After 3 weeks, remove one salami and weigh it. The minimum weight loss should be 30 percent; however, you should target a 40-percent weight loss for a firm salami.

22 If you have reached the proper weight loss, pack your salamis into a vacuum bag and let them rest under vacuum for 30 days to ensure there is no case hardening.

TIP: Using just a little of your grind, stuff a very small sausage, called a *chub*. You will use the chub to test the pH of the salamis.

TIP: Use single-use food-safe gloves for this entire process. Change them often.

WARNING: You are making an uncooked, fermented, ready-to-eat sausage. Hygiene and sanitation are critical to staying safe and managing possible contamination. Clean and sanitize often.

Truffle Salami

PREP TIME: 1 HOUR + 1 DAY	FERMENTATION TIME: 2–3 DAYS	DRYING TIME: 3–6 WEEKS

INGREDIENTS

45 grams (2%) sea salt

6 grams (.25%) pink salt #2

10 grams (.45%) coarse ground black pepper

10 grams (.45%) dextrose

22 grams (1%) minced garlic

45 grams (2%) black truffle oil

½ teaspoon Bactoferm F-RM-52 starter culture

4 oz. distilled water

4 lbs. boneless pork shoulder

1 lb. pork back fat (or pork belly)

Beef middles, fully hydrated and flushed

1 Combine all of the dry ingredients and garlic in a mixing bowl and set aside.

2 Combine the distilled water and Bactoferm starter culture in a dish and set aside.

3 Cut the pork shoulder and pork fat / pork belly into pieces small enough to fit into your grinder.

4 In a large mixing bowl or food-safe plastic tub, combine the dry ingredients with the protein and fat. Mix thoroughly.

5 Place the seasoned meat mixture into the freezer for an hour.

6 Place the grinder head and #3/16" plate into the freezer for an hour.

7 Assemble the grinder head with the #3/16" plate.

8 Grind the seasoned meat mixture into a large bowl.

9 Add the black truffle oil.

10 Add the starter culture and water mixture.

11 Mix the ground sausage with your hands for 2 minutes.

12 Press the mixture into the bowl bottom and cover the mixture with plastic wrap. Get all of the air out.

13 Refrigerate the mixture overnight.

14 Cut your beef middles into 8-inch sections. Tie one end of each piece using a square knot (refer to Chapter 4 if you need a refresher).

(continued)

15 Stuff the sausage, fully and tightly, into the beef middles. Once you tie the untied end, you will want the sausage casing to spring back when pressed with your finger.

16 Prick the sausage casing to ensure no air bubbles exist.

17 Spray the sausages with your mold spray (refer to the earlier section, "Molding the Next Generation of Salami," in this chapter).

18 Place the sausages into your fermentation chamber at 70 degrees Fahrenheit and 90-percent humidity. (If you do not have a chamber, refer to the fermentation section in this chapter for alternative options for fermentation.)

19 After 48 hours of fermentation, remove the chub and test it with your pH meter. If the pH is 5.1 or lower, you are ready to dry. If it is not yet at 5.1, allow it to continue fermenting for another 48 hours. Re-test. If it is not below 5.1 at this point, there may have been something wrong with your starter culture. Discard your salamis and start again.

20 Hang your sausages in your drying chamber. Set the temperature to a high threshold of 55 degrees Fahrenheit and a low threshold of 50 degrees Fahrenheit. Set the humidity to 75 percent. Walk away and let your sausages hang for a minimum of 3 weeks.

21 After 3 weeks, remove one salami and weigh it. The minimum weight loss should be 30 percent; however, you should target a 40-percent weight loss for a firm salami.

22 If you have reached the proper weight loss, pack your salamis into a vacuum bag and let them rest under vacuum for 30 days to ensure there is no case hardening.

TIP: Using just a little of your grind, stuff a very small sausage, called a *chub*. You will use the chub to test the pH of the salamis.

TIP: Use single-use food-safe gloves for this entire process. Change them often.

WARNING: You are making an uncooked, fermented, ready-to-eat sausage. Hygiene and sanitation are critical to staying safe and managing possible contamination. Clean and sanitize often.

Orange Zest Salami

PREP TIME: 1 HOUR + 1 DAY	FERMENTATION TIME: 2-3 DAYS	DRYING TIME: 3-6 WEEKS

INGREDIENTS

45 grams (2%) sea salt

6 grams (.25%) pink salt #2

4 grams (.2%) crushed red pepper

10 grams (.45%) dextrose

45 grams (2%) fresh orange zest

8 grams (.33%) coarse ground black pepper

28 grams (1.25%) minced garlic

34 grams (1.5%) Grand Marnier

½ teaspoon Bactoferm F-RM-52 starter culture

4 oz. distilled water

4 lbs. boneless pork shoulder

1 lb. pork back fat (or pork belly)

Beef middles, fully hydrated and flushed

1 Combine all of the dry ingredients, orange zest, and garlic in a mixing bowl and set aside.

2 Combine the distilled water and Bactoferm starter culture in a dish and set aside.

3 Cut the pork shoulder and pork fat / pork belly into pieces small enough to fit into your grinder.

4 In a large mixing bowl or food-safe plastic tub, combine the dry ingredients with the protein and fat. Mix thoroughly.

5 Place the seasoned meat mixture into the freezer for an hour.

6 Place the grinder head and #3/16" plate into the freezer for an hour.

7 Assemble the grinder head with the #3/16" plate.

8 Grind the seasoned meat mixture into a large bowl.

9 Add the Grand Marnier.

10 Add the starter culture and water mixture.

11 Mix the ground sausage with your hands for 2 minutes.

12 Press the mixture into the bowl bottom and cover the mixture with plastic wrap. Get all of the air out.

13 Refrigerate the mixture overnight.

14 Cut your beef middles into 8-inch sections. Tie one end of each piece using a square knot (refer to Chapter 4 if you need a refresher).

(continued)

15 Stuff the sausage, fully and tightly, into the beef middles. Once you tie the untied end, you will want the sausage casing to spring back when pressed with your finger.

16 Prick the sausage casing to ensure no air bubbles exist.

17 Spray the sausages with your mold spray (refer to the earlier section, "Molding the Next Generation of Salami," in this chapter).

18 Place the sausages into your fermentation chamber at 70 degrees Fahrenheit and 90-percent humidity. (If you do not have a chamber, refer to the fermentation section in this chapter for alternative options for fermentation.)

19 After 48 hours of fermentation, remove the chub and test it with your pH meter. If the pH is 5.1 or lower, you are ready to dry. If it is not yet at 5.1, allow it to continue fermenting for another 48 hours. Re-test. If it is not below 5.1 at this point, there may have been something wrong with your starter culture. Discard your salamis and start again.

20 Hang your sausages in your drying chamber. Set the temperature to a high threshold of 55 degrees Fahrenheit and a low threshold of 50 degrees Fahrenheit. Set the humidity to 75 percent. Walk away and let your sausages hang for a minimum of 3 weeks.

21 After 3 weeks, remove one salami and weigh it. The minimum weight loss should be 30 percent; however, you should target a 40-percent weight loss for a firm salami.

22 If you have reached the proper weight loss, pack your salamis into a vacuum bag and let them rest under vacuum for 30 days to ensure there is no case hardening.

TIP: Using just a little of your grind, stuff a very small sausage, called a *chub*. You will use the chub to test the pH of the salamis.

TIP: Use single-use food-safe gloves for this entire process. Change them often.

WARNING: You are making an uncooked, fermented, ready-to-eat sausage. Hygiene and sanitation are critical to staying safe and managing possible contamination. Clean and sanitize often.

Milano-Style Salami

PREP TIME: 1 HOUR + 1 DAY	FERMENTATION TIME: 2–3 DAYS	DRYING TIME: 3–6 WEEKS

INGREDIENTS

45 grams (2%) sea salt

6 grams (.25%) pink salt #2

10 grams (.45%) cracked black pepper

28 grams (1.25%) minced garlic

10 grams (.45%) ground white pepper

6 grams (.25%) ground nutmeg

10 grams (.45%) dextrose

½ teaspoon Bactoferm F-RM-52 starter culture

4 oz. distilled water

4 lbs. boneless pork shoulder

1 lb. pork back fat (or pork belly)

Beef middles, fully hydrated and flushed

1 Combine all of the dry ingredients in a mixing bowl and set aside.

2 Combine the distilled water and Bactoferm starter culture in a dish and set aside.

3 Cut the pork shoulder and pork fat / pork belly into pieces small enough to fit into your grinder.

4 In a large mixing bowl or food-safe plastic tub, combine the dry ingredients with the protein and fat. Mix thoroughly.

5 Place the seasoned meat mixture into the freezer for an hour.

6 Place the grinder head and #3/16" plate into the freezer for an hour.

7 Assemble the grinder head with the #3/16" plate.

8 Grind the seasoned meat mixture into a large bowl.

9 Add the starter culture and water mixture.

10 Mix the ground sausage with your hands for 2 minutes.

11 Press the mixture into the bowl bottom and cover the mixture with plastic wrap. Get all of the air out.

12 Refrigerate the mixture overnight.

13 Cut your beef middles into 8-inch sections. Tie one end of each piece using a square knot (refer to Chapter 4 if you need a refresher).

(continued)

14 Stuff the sausage, fully and tightly, into the beef middles. Once you tie the untied end, you will want the sausage casing to spring back when pressed with your finger.

15 Prick the sausage casing to ensure no air bubbles exist.

16 Spray the sausages with your mold spray (refer to the earlier section, "Molding the Next Generation of Salami," in this chapter).

17 Place the sausages into your fermentation chamber at 70 degrees Fahrenheit and 90-percent humidity. (If you do not have a chamber, refer to the fermentation section in this chapter for alternative options for fermentation.)

18 After 48 hours of fermentation, remove the chub and test it with your pH meter. If the pH is 5.1 or lower, you are ready to dry. If it is not yet at 5.1, allow it to continue fermenting for another 48 hours. Re-test. If it is not below 5.1 at this point, there may have been something wrong with your starter culture. Discard your salamis and start again.

19 Hang your sausages in your drying chamber. Set the temperature to a high threshold of 55 degrees Fahrenheit and a low threshold of 50 degrees Fahrenheit. Set the humidity to 75 percent. Walk away and let your sausages hang for a minimum of 3 weeks.

20 After 3 weeks, remove one salami and weigh it. The minimum weight loss should be 30 percent; however, you should target a 40-percent weight loss for a firm salami.

21 If you have reached the proper weight loss, pack your salamis into a vacuum bag and let them rest under vacuum for 30 days to ensure there is no case hardening.

TIP: Using just a little of your grind, stuff a very small sausage, called a *chub*. You will use the chub to test the pH of the salamis.

TIP: Use single-use food-safe gloves for this entire process. Change them often.

WARNING: You are making an uncooked, fermented, ready-to-eat sausage. Hygiene and sanitation are critical to staying safe and managing possible contamination. Clean and sanitize often.

3
Entertaining with Charcuterie

Chapter **8**

Always the Entertainer

People who love to eat are always the best people.

— JULIA CHILD

I find it interesting that very early on, charcuterie was something that the afflu-ent would turn their noses up to. Can you imagine that? Whoever those people were, they missed out on one of life's true pleasures. Aged, dry-cured meats have a depth of flavor like nothing in this world, a natural umami that is mesmer-izing if not intoxicating. These delicious bits take an exceptional amount of time and care to produce, and the true artisan's skill shines through in the end product. Thankfully, the perception of charcuterie has evolved over time and was not snuffed out by the grossly uninformed aristocracy.

Charcuterie's place in the modern culinary world has actually become elevated. In fact, the craft of dry-curing meats of all types has entered a renaissance period. A technique that was once simply a way of survival has become a food experience in and of itself. Charcuterie boards grace the menus of some of the world's most prestigious restaurants. These boards are creation stations where your guests choose from an assortment of meats and pair them with cheeses, assorted pickles, dried fruits, mustards, toast, and so much more to create unique bites. It is no wonder that charcuterie boards have become ubiquitous in entertaining.

What's even better? You don't have to have a degree in hospitality or the culinary arts to blow your guests' minds with charcuterie. In this chapter you will get a primer on the various ingredients for making an incredible charcuterie board that will impress your guests. You will get tips and ideas on where to find the best products, how to incorporate different types of cheese, and the accouterment that will take each bite from good to great. At the end of this chapter, you will find some simple recipes for spreads, pickles, and other assorted ingredients that will paint an "S" on your chest!

Sourcing Great Proteins

Never forget that charcuterie is first and foremost a word used to describe dry-cured meat, not a spread of meat, cheese, and pickles. So when you start thinking about what you want to put on your charcuterie board, do what I do and start your planning with the meat. There is an ocean of options out there and you will need to filter through them to find the gems, but that's part of the fun, isn't it? In the last 20 years, charcuterie has gained popularity in the United States. Quite a few self-taught folks are making great things, although upon occasion, you will find some not-so-great stuff. Following is a list of some domestic products that I tend to gravitate toward because they are awesome:

>> Brooklyn Cured

>> Creminelli

>> Elevation

>> Fra' Mani

>> La Quercia

>> 'Nduja Artisans

>> Nueske's

>> Olympia Provisions

>> River Bear

>> Smoking Goose

When you are trying to find delicious meats for your spread, believe it or not, several options are at your disposal unless you live in the middle of nowhere. But even there, the NSA and, more importantly, Amazon.com, can find you. Following are a couple of options for places to find the ingredients for your charcuterie board masterpiece.

>> **Artisanal butcher shop / gourmet grocery:** In Indianapolis we have several small shops where you can find quality ingredients for a killer spread. My

default is a shop called Goose the Market. The great thing about Goose the Market, and other butcher / artisanal grocers like them, is that they have a wide selection of meats in the deli case that can be sliced and sampled (see Figure 8-1). If you're unsure of what to get, their staff are well informed and can help you make some great selections. Another benefit is that you can usually find products that are not mass-produced and, especially in the case of Goose the Market, you can find some of their own creations.

FIGURE 8-1:
Goose the Market
deli case.

Corrie E. Cook for Goose the Market and Smoking Goose

>> **Big box "specialty" grocery:** If you don't have an artisanal butcher shop or gourmet grocer nearby, you could also check out a big box store like Fresh Thyme, The Fresh Market, Market District, Whole Foods Market, or something similar. These stores have larger selections than the typical grocery store. One drawback is that the options will largely be pre-packaged and if you are unfamiliar with the offerings, you won't have the option to try before you buy.

TIP

Trader Joe's is my secret weapon for assembling all the pieces you'll need for a killer spread. Their cheese selection is quite extensive given the size of that section of the store. Their cured meats are limited but are generally of a decent quality, and the options for accouterments are plentiful.

Wherever you find your products, whether in a store or online, make sure that what you are buying is fresh. I know it sounds crazy to call something that is aged for flavor "fresh," but like all things, consuming closer to the package best-by date is ideal. Freshness is imperative if you are buying something pre-sliced. Oftentimes meats like prosciutto, capicola, coppa, and various salamis can come pre-packaged and sliced. These meats will go stale more quickly than meats that are unsliced, so be sure to check the package and best-by date.

There is no hard and fast rule to how many meats to purchase for your board. Personally, I always try to have at least two whole muscle options like coppa and prosciutto. Thinly sliced salamis can help fill out the board with additional options. You can also add some fattier items like thin slices of guanciale, which goes wonderfully wrapped around a marcona almond. If you want some textural variation, and you think your guests would be interested, pate and rillettes are both a nice spreadable option.

Say Cheese

This book talks a lot about a variety of meats, but if meat is the king of the charcuterie board, then cheese is the queen. Long live the queen. I've often thought that I could live on cheese and bread; however, my doctor has advised strongly against it. I can't imagine that anyone needs an introduction to cheese, but here it is: Cheese is a dairy product derived from milk. It comes in all sorts of shapes, sizes, textures, smells, flavors, and so on. In theory, you can make cheese from any animal's milk. (Cue the *Meet the Parents* quote.)

The majority of cheeses come from the milk of cows, buffalo, goats, and sheep. An ocean of detailed information could be written about the cheeses of the world, what makes them unique, the science behind them, the process of making them, and so on. For the purposes of this book, I won't delve too far into the topic, but after this section you should have enough information to confidently select cheeses for your charcuterie board!

Cheese is a natural accompaniment to a charcuterie board because it provides additional flavor and texture to the mix. Cheese and meat go together like peanut butter and jelly, but cheese also gracefully bridges the gap between savory and sweet. There are many different ways to categorize cheese: milk type, firmness, rind type, and so on. For the sake of variety on a charcuterie board, I tend to focus on firmness first. Firmness of a cheese is determined by moisture content. The higher the moisture content, the softer the cheese, and vice versa. The categories of firmness range from soft to hard, and a great deal of diversity can be found in each of these categories. Let's take a look at some of the nuances of each.

Soft and semi-soft cheese

Soft cheese has the highest amount of moisture content. For this reason, these cheeses tend to have the shortest shelf life. Many (if not all) soft cheeses do not have the whey completely pressed out of them, and this is what helps give them a creamy texture. Many soft cheeses should be served at room temperature so that they are soft, if not slightly runny, and thus easy to spread. The cheese will be more fragrant and flavorful at room temperature as well. I always try to have at least one if not two soft cheeses on a board. Even if you are entertaining a small group, you can use smaller pieces, but a little variety from this group is great. Following are some of my favorite soft cheeses.

>> **Brie:** Shown in Figure 8-2, Brie is a soft, spreadable creamy cheese that originated in France. In fact, the authentic French version cannot be imported to the U.S. because it is made with raw milk. The rind is soft and edible, and usually has a light coating of white penicillin mold. Brie has a wonderful, creamy texture and a slightly earthy flavor. It goes great with fig jam and salty meats.

FIGURE 8-2:
Brie cheese.

Photo by David Pluimer

>> **Époisses de Bourgogne:** This is a cheese that has legal protection for its name and method of production. It comes from the village of Époisses in the Burgundy region of France. This is a soft cheese that is hand washed with local brandy as it ages. It is a pungent cheese with bold flavors and a creamy texture. Hints of bitterness make this a good pair with sweeter flavors.

>> **Saint-André:** This is a delicious cheese made in the Normandy region of France. It is fortified with cream, which gives it a very high fat content and a very dense, rich, buttery flavor. Saint-André goes well with savory items like roasted nuts, or sweet companions like dried cherry or cranberry, and possibly some jam or candied nuts.

>> **Foxglove:** There is a creamery in Indianapolis called Tulip Tree (www.tuliptreecreamery.com) that makes several European-style cheeses; one of their soft cheeses is called Foxglove (see Figure 8-3). I love this cheese because it is almost like a mild talleggio. It has a light-orange rind that can be eaten. The inside is soft and spongy when young, but as it ages and ripens, it becomes creamier and more spreadable. This is a bold, pungent cheese that goes great with salty nuts, dried fruits, and salty meats.

>> **Blue Stilton:** Probably my mother's favorite cheese, Stilton is an English cheese that can be either white or blue. The blue color comes from a specific type of mold that is intentionally incorporated into the cheese, and provides some unique nutty and fruity characteristics to the cheese. Stilton must be made in the village of Stilton in the United Kingdom. It is not as soft as the other cheeses in this list, but it is relatively spreadable as it approaches room temperature. Stilton pairs well with fresh apples, pears, dried fruits, and honey.

FIGURE 8-3:
Foxglove cheese.

Photo by David Pluimer

Medium-hard cheese

Medium-hard cheeses can range from semi-soft to firm. Cheeses in this category have a nice balance in moisture content, which gives them a firm, slightly springy texture. Generally speaking, cheeses in this category have been aged less than six months. They have some fresh flavors blended in with some developed character-istics. You can grate these cheeses, and they are generally ideal for melting. The older medium-hard cheeses are pretty easy to slice cleanly. When I am putting together a charcuterie board, I will use one or two medium-hard cheeses. Some-times if I use two, I will opt to not use any *hard* cheeses. Some of my favorite medium-hard cheeses include the following.

>> **Vermont sharp cheddar:** Cheddar originated in the United Kingdom; however, it has made its way over to the U.S. where several creameries have made their own versions of this world-famous cheese. Cabot Creamery in Vermont makes an aged cheddar that is righteous, and I often like to include it on my charcuterie boards. Cabot Artisan Reserve three-year-aged cheddar is a sharp, delicious cheese that pairs well with dried fruits, salty meats, fresh apples, and plums.

>> **Gouda:** Pronounced "how-duh" not "goo-da," Gouda (see Figure 8-4) is mild cheese that originates from The Netherlands. The name is not protected, and so you can find Gouda made all over the world in a number of different ways. You can find Dutch Gouda as young as four weeks old and as aged as over a year old. It has a lovely, mild, nutty flavor, and sometimes a sweet fruitiness can be detected. Gouda goes well with salty meats, dried fruits, and nuts.

FIGURE 8-4:
Gouda cheese.

Photo by David Pluimer

>> **Manchego:** This is a Spanish cheese originating in the La Mancha region and made from the milk of Manchega sheep. Manchego cheese (shown in Figure 8-5) can range from 60 days young to upwards of two years old. It has a mild flavor and a slightly creamy texture. Some Manchego can have a detectible spice, and it can have a slightly tart aftertaste indicative of sheep's milk. This cheese is ideal for pairing with nuts, savory tomatoes, dried fruits, honey, and olive oil.

>> **Gruyère:** Named after the Swiss town, Gruyère is a delightful cheese that is actually quite nice melted over bread. It has a mild, creamy texture that is rich, buttery, and slightly nutty. Gruyère can have some small "eyes" in the cheese from the bacteria that is used to make the cheese. However this is not a typical Swiss cheese that is filled with bubbles of all sizes. Gruyère is versatile and can be paired with fruits, nuts, mustards, and all meats.

FIGURE 8-5:
Manchego
cheese.

Photo by David Pluimer

Hard cheese

Hard cheeses have the lowest moisture content of all the cheeses. These cheeses are generally pressed and molded firmly to squeeze out much of the moisture at the onset of aging. They can be aged much longer, sometimes for years! Many medium-hard cheeses can also be aged longer to become classified as hard cheeses.

One thing that I love about hard cheeses is that they can really show off the minerals of a cheese. In some aged pecorino, Parmesan, and aged Gouda, small bits of mineral crystals will form in the cheese, giving it a really cool textural nuance. While I prefer hard cheese, I try to use only one on a charcuterie board. They can be stronger in flavor and do not have the broader appeal of the younger cheeses. Following are some of my favorite hard cheeses.

» **Aged Pecorino Romano:** Pecorino originates from Italy, and the name is given to cheeses made from 100-percent sheep's milk. Aged Pecorino Romano is a very hard cheese with a really cool texture that is crumbly at first and then melts as it warms in your mouth. Small bits of mineral deposits throughout the aged cheese give it a bit of textural variation as you crunch into them. The cheese is very nutty, buttery in flavor, and has hints of black peppercorn. This cheese is great with savory, earthy items, nuts, and honey.

» **Cave-aged Gouda:** This is Gouda that is first aged for 3 to 6 months prior to being relocated to a cave to age further. The cave provides a moist, cool environment that can impart all sorts of different unique and delicious qualities to the Gouda as it goes through an extended aging period. The finished product is a complex cheese that is quite firm. The flavors are rich and more developed than in its younger version. It has a more pronounced nutty flavor, minerals are more present, and darker flavors like caramel start to emerge. Pair with honey, nuts, salty meats, and sweet, dried fruits.

» **Merlot BellaVitano:** This is an American-made cheese that is the brainchild of the Sartori Company of Wisconsin. The cheese, pictured in Figure 8-6, is inspired by Parmesan but it is quite different nonetheless. This is a hard cheese that is pressed and formed into a wheel for aging. It has a creamy, rich texture with crunchy mineral crystals that form in the cheese as it matures. It is washed in Merlot wine as it ages, which gives the rind a unique purple hue. This cheese is great with salty meats, olives, and nuts. At family events, we eat it by the pound.

FIGURE 8-6:
Merlot
BellaVitano.

Photo by David Pluimer

Condiments and Accouterments

No charcuterie board is complete with just meat and cheese. There are several other small ingredients that can fill out your charcuterie board and provide fantastic accompaniments to your meats and cheeses. Your goal isn't to build sandwiches, but rather to provide small components that your guests can use to make several unique, small bites. This will provide another aspect of enjoyment as they explore and try different things. Following is a handful of ways that you can dress up your charcuterie board to really impress!

>> **Mustards and spreads:** I love mustard. Not the ballpark neon-yellow stuff, but the real thing. I love a good Dijon mustard, whole-grain, spicy, mellow, you name it. In my opinion you can't go wrong with a good mustard for your charcuterie board. A whole-grain, Dijon-style mustard, pictured in Figure 8-7, like Maille is my go-to. However, numerous delicious mustards are available from other smaller producers. In Indianapolis we have a great boutique sauce company called Batch No. 2. They make many different types of mustards that are fantastic. Mustards are a great accompaniment to sausages, such as whole-muscle, dry-cured eats like prosciutto, coppa, and capicola. The acidity in mustard is fantastic for cutting fatty bites. I also love whole-grain mustard with pâté on a cracker or toast.

FIGURE 8-7: Whole-grain mustard.

Photo by David Pluimer

In addition to mustards, give some consideration to other fun spreads like olive tapenade, which is a finely minced mixture of briny olives with olive oil and spices. Savory tomato jam is a nice, vibrant addition to any charcuterie board because it provides a deep, complex, savory flavor that is offset with some acidity and slight sweetness in the aftertaste. Use mustards, savory jams, and tapenades with salted meats that don't have a lot of additional spices so you don't get conflicting flavors.

>> **Jams and marmalades:** If you go savory non-stop, then at some point your palate will get tired and everything will begin to taste the same. Sweet things are a great way to press Reset. Jams and marmalades, pictured in Figure 8-8, pair nicely with cheeses. For example, try fig jam with Brie, Camembert, or goat cheese; apricot jam with Parmesan or Brie; blackberry or pear jam with Stilton Blue; blueberry jam with Manchego; or orange marmalade with Gouda.

No good jam or marmalade? Honey goes great with almost everything.

TIP

FIGURE 8-8:
Assorted jams and marmalade.

Photo by David Pluimer

>> **Pickles:** I love a good pickle. Not just dill pickle spears or coins, but pickled anything. Sour pickles can provide a great accompaniment to fatty meats, spreads, and cheeses. They can be paired with other accouterments or used to cleanse the palate. You can use sweet pickles in the same manner. Small baby pickles (also called cornichons), when cut in half, are the perfect size and flavor to go with pâté. Crunch on one or two with some dried meats and mustard. Pickled shallots add a nice onion flavor to any meat, and acid from the vinegar brine will cut through the fat. Making quick pickles in the fridge is a great way to introduce really unique pickles. Have you ever had pickled watermelon rind?

>> **Olives:** I love olives, in all shapes, sizes, and flavors. They also come in all levels of salty, with different herbs and spices to provide accents. My go-to olives are Castelvetrano. These are large, light-green olives that have a mild flavor and are packed in a lighter brine. They are nicknamed "butter olives" because of their flavor and texture. If Castelvetrano olives are wrong, I don't ever want to be right!

>> **Dried fruits and nuts:** Fruits and nuts provide a nice texture and flavor variation to everything else on a charcuterie board. Whole nuts like pecans, almonds, and walnuts offer nice, mild flavors to accent numerous cheeses. Dried apricots, cherries, and cranberries are fantastic with dried nuts and cheese. Their sweetness isn't overwhelming and it provides a little relief from the salty, savory options. I love Marcona almonds because they are like a cross between an almond and a cashew. Figure 8-9 is a pile of marcona almonds. Consider dressing up nuts by roasting them in butter and different herbs, or go the sweet route and try candying them. I like the combination of candied pecan with cayenne pepper.

>> **Crackers and bread:** Unless you want your guests to behave like complete savages, you should have some crackers and bread available for building bites. I like water crackers for most things because, being a blank palette, they are truly just a delivery mechanism. You can get quite fancy with your bread. Try slicing baguettes on the bias, top with olive oil, toast in the oven, sprinkle a little sea salt on top, and you've got a great option for a little mustard and prosciutto. Or maybe try some flavored crackers. Trader Joe's has a fig cracker that goes swimmingly with Brie. Make sure you have plenty of bread, toast, or crackers so that your guests can make as many bites as necessary! Place them strategically in multiple places on your charcuterie board.

FIGURE 8-9:
Marcona
almonds.

Photo by David Pluimer

Bringing It All Together!

Picking out the different meats, cheeses, and accouterment is one of my favorite parts of putting together a charcuterie board. Selection, however, is just the beginning. You want to be able to properly estimate the volume of each item to buy. Then you get to channel your inner artist by selecting the type of platter or board to use and then organizing all the tasty eats!

Proper portioning

Picking out all of the ingredients for your charcuterie board is a lot of fun, but it can also be the most hectic part of the process if you are faced with a ton of options! I consider the most difficult part of shopping for a charcuterie board to be getting the portions right. You don't want to over-buy for your event, but you also don't want to under-buy. It's okay if your board gets picked clean, but you don't want that to happen too early in the evening. To ensure that you get the right amount, you really need to understand the purpose that your charcuterie course is going to serve.

If you are intending to make the charcuterie board the main attraction, then you will need to go heavy on your portioning. If your charcuterie board is meant to be an appetizer, then you will want to go lighter. If you are having a multi-course meal, or if you are planning to set out a buffet for dinner, then you will want to go extra light. Following are some meat-and-cheese portion guidelines for your charcuterie board to help you shop.

>> **As the main attraction:** Plan to purchase 2 to 2.5 ounces of meat and 2 to 2.5 ounces of cheese per person.

>> **As an appetizer:** Plan to purchase 1.5 to 2 ounces of meat and 1 to 1.5 ounces of cheese per person.

>> **As part of a multi-course meal or buffet:** Plan to purchase 1 ounce of meat and 1 ounce of cheese per person.

The accouterment is not as easy to portion out formulaically because these selections will be relative to your balance of meat and cheese. Also, when purchasing mustards, jams, nuts, and so on, you don't get as much flexibility in volumes of the containers.

The platter

At this point you should have all of your meats, cheeses, pickles, nuts, snacks, jams, crackers, and bread picked out and ready to be arranged on your board. But before you can do that, you need to get your board ready! While I use the word "board" universally to describe the platter on which charcuterie is arranged, you don't actually have to use a board. This word is heavily favored largely due to charcuterie and cheeses being cut and served on a cutting board. You can, however, use whatever serving platter suits you!

I've seen remarkable spreads on ceramic platters, slate tiles, and sanded and finished barn wood. A few years ago, my friend Eric removed a large, black walnut tree from a property on which he was building a house. Thankfully he saved the tree and had it milled down into boards for use in all sorts of unique applications within the homes he was building at the time. I managed to talk him out of a couple of really large pieces that I later sanded and sealed with food-grade mineral oil to make some really cool boards for charcuterie. The first one is four feet long and so it was lovingly called the "Four Feet of Meat." The second board is thicker and heavier but came after the Four Feet of Meat, and so we referred to it as "son of meat." Take a look at the Four Feet of Meat board in Figure 8-10.

FIGURE 8-10:
The "Four Feet of Meat"

Photo by David Pluimer

You don't need an extravagant board to present your delicious spread, but going a little over the top in this area won't hurt you!

Arranging your board

Arranging everything on the charcuterie board is an art. You can get as creative as you want with this step. If you spend any time on Pinterest, odds are good that you can find some very extravagantly made charcuterie boards. But if you aren't the Picasso of meat and cheese, never fear.

The most important part is that you arrange everything so as to lead your guests toward the combinations you want them to try. For example, don't put the Brie by the mustard; put it next to the jam. Maybe don't put the pickles next to a pile of nuts, but rather next to a pâté or sausage. This way, as your guests are picking items out for their plate, they don't have to think too much about the combinations to try. Refer to the earlier section, "Condiments and Accouterments," to get some ideas of what to place near what.

Once you have a general idea of where you want things to go, you have a few options of how to lay out your board. Following are a couple of different methods named after some good friends of mine.

>> **The Dooley:** My good friend Tim likes to take all of his meats and align them in perfectly straight rows. In between the meats, he places his cheeses and then in perfect, nice little piles he places nuts and dried fruits. Crackers and crostini go in straight lines, and mustard, pickles, olives, and jams go in their own little containers and are placed in symmetrical order. Figure 8-11 illustrates the place and order of the Dooley charcuterie board.

>> **The Stoneking:** My friend Josh likes to place nice, neat piles of organized chaos around a board. Slices of prosciutto are scrunched up to form voluminous piles of protein. Thin slices of hard salami are arranged in neat piles. Crackers and crostini are piled up in different areas of the board. Pickles, jams, mustards, and the like are placed so as to create visual balance. Figure 8-12 illustrates Josh's style accurately.

No matter how you arrange your board, make sure that you place complementary items near each other.

FIGURE 8-11:
The Dooley.

Mark LaFay

FIGURE 8-12:
The Stoneking.

Photo by David Pluimer

Quick Pickle Chips

|

INGREDIENTS

1–2 cucumbers

1 cup rice vinegar

1 cup distilled water

1 tablespoon kosher salt or sea salt

1 teaspoon sugar

1 teaspoon whole allspice

1 teaspoon whole peppercorn

1 teaspoon crushed red pepper flakes

1 tablespoon fresh dill fronds

2 peeled garlic cloves

1 Wash your cucumber under cool water, being sure to get any residue or debris off the outside.

2 Slice the cucumber to make 1/8- to 1/4-inch coins.

3 Place cucumber coins into a non-reactive stainless-steel or glass bowl, or a mason jar.

4 Using the side of a chef's knife, smash the garlic cloves.

5 In a small pot, combine the water, vinegar, salt, sugar, spices, and fresh garlic.

6 Over medium heat, stir the mixture until the salt and sugar have fully dissolved into the solution.

7 Pour the mixture into your bowl or mason jar of cucumbers.

8 Seal and refrigerate the mixture for 24 hours.

9 Sample a cucumber coin to see if it is sour enough; if not, let them sit for another day or two.

TIP: Mix up the spices to get different flavors in the pickles, or go with no spices and just do a slightly sour cucumber. You can also try swapping out the cucumber for a different vegetable.

WARNING: This pickle recipe must be refrigerated; only store it in the fridge. It will last indefinitely if refrigerated; however, you will experience a loss in quality over time, so use it sooner than later.

Pickled Shallot

INGREDIENTS

2 cups sliced shallot

1 cup rice vinegar

1 cup distilled water

1 tablespoon kosher salt or sea salt

1 teaspoon sugar

Small pinch of dry thyme

1 Wash and clean your shallots.

2 Slice the shallots 1/16 inch thick.

3 Place the shallots in a non-reactive stainless steel or glass bowl, or a mason jar.

4 In a small pot, combine the water, vinegar, salt, sugar, and thyme.

5 Over medium heat, stir the mixture until the salt and sugar have fully dissolved into the solution.

6 Combine the brine mixture with the sliced shallots in the bowl or mason jar.

7 Refrigerate for 24 hours.

8 Sample a shallot to see if it is sour enough; if not, let them sit for another day or two.

TIP: Mix up the spices to get different flavors in the shallot. Shallots are a great accent to a charcuterie board, so try not to overpower the natural flavor of the shallot with too much additional spice.

WARNING: This shallot recipe must be refrigerated; only store it in the fridge. It will last indefinitely if refrigerated; however, you will experience a loss in quality over time, so use it sooner than later.

Truffle Popcorn

INGREDIENTS

3 tablespoons coconut oil

1/3 cup high-quality popcorn kernels

5 tablespoons unsalted, grass-fed or European-style butter

2 tablespoons truffle oil

1 cup Parmesan cheese (freshly grated)

Sea salt to taste

Black pepper

1 Place a deep pot on the stove and turn the heat on medium high. Add the coconut oil.

2 Melt the coconut oil completely, and then add the popcorn to the pot and put a lid on the pot.

3 Shake the pot periodically and listen for the kernels to begin popping.

4 Once the kernels have thoroughly popped, remove them from the heat and toss the popcorn into an oversized mixing bowl.

5 Using a microplane, finely grate your Parmesan cheese. If you can't find Parmesan, pecorino will work too.

6 In a glass dish, melt 5 tablespoons of butter in a microwave oven.

7 Combine the truffle oil and butter.

8 Lightly dress the popcorn with all of the truffle oil and butter mixture. Toss the popcorn as you are combining it so that you get an even distribution.

9 Sprinkle the Parmesan cheese over the popcorn, tossing the popcorn to ensure an even distribution.

10 Taste the popcorn and then add salt and pepper to your preference.

11 Try not to eat it all.

TIP: Do not heat the truffle oil with the butter. Truffle is a very sensitive flavor and can cook off.

TIP: Don't cheap out on the cheese. Ground Kraft Parmesan is not acceptable.

TIP: Don't cheap out on the butter. Shame on you if you use margarine.

Savory Tomato Jam

PREP TIME: 90 MINUTES

INGREDIENTS

2 lbs. mixture of cherry, grape, and pear tomatoes

3 tablespoons olive oil

⅔ cup champagne vinegar (rice vinegar if you can't find champagne vinegar)

1 large shallot

4 large, peeled garlic cloves

¾ cup white sugar

Zest of 1 lemon

2 tablespoons sea salt

1   Wash and clean your tomatoes. Set them aside.

2   Finely mince the garlic and shallot. Set it aside.

3   Zest the lemon. Set it aside.

4   Place a large saucepan on the stove and set the heat to medium. Add the olive oil, garlic, and shallot.

5   Sweat the shallot and garlic, but do not burn or caramelize them.

6   Add the tomatoes and cook them down. As they heat up, they will split and start rendering their liquids. You can speed this along by gently breaking the tomatoes in the pan.

7   Reduce the tomatoes into a sauce and add the vinegar, sugar, and salt.

8   Continue reducing the tomato mixture.

9   Add the lemon zest.

10   Reduce the mixture until it is quite thick. Be sure to continually stir so that it does not burn.

You will know your mixture is ready if you drag a spoon or spatula across the bottom of the pan and the mixture slowly spreads back out, covering the pan space revealed by dragging your spoon across the pan.

11   Using a rubber spatula, scrape all of the hot jam into a mason jar or bowl. Cover with plastic wrap and refrigerate.

TIP: If you want a finer texture, purée the tomatoes prior to adding them to the saucepan. Then reduce.

TIP: You can use all grape or all cherry tomatoes; however, using a blend will give you a more interesting finished flavor.

REMEMBER: Keep the jam refrigerated.

Rosemary Toasted Marcona Almonds

PREP TIME: 30 MINUTES

INGREDIENTS

3 tablespoons unsalted, grass-fed butter, or olive oil

1 tablespoon dry rosemary

1 cup Marcona almonds

Sea salt to taste

1 Place a frying pan on the stove and set the heat to medium.

2 Add the butter, and heat it until melted.

3 Add the dry rosemary. Let the warming butter heat the rosemary to extract the flavors.

4 When the milk solids in the melted butter begin to brown, add the Marcona almonds to the pan.

5 Toss the mixture until the almonds are covered in butter and rosemary. Toast the almonds.

6 Sprinkle on the sea salt to taste.

7 Put the almonds into a serving dish and place them on your charcuterie board.

VARY IT! Try other dry spices like thyme, cayenne, black pepper, and so on.

VARY IT! Make truffle Marcona almonds by toasting them with butter and then sprinkling them with truffle salt.

Chapter **9**

Wine and Charcuterie

In wine there is wisdom, in beer there is freedom, in water there is bacteria.
— BENJAMIN FRANKLIN

I didn't really start exploring the world of wine until I was nearing my late 20s. Don't get me wrong; I would drink wine, I had no aversion to it, but it wasn't until some friends popped a few nice bottles in my presence that my eyes were opened to what wine could be. When I was nearing 30, my wife and I ventured to Napa Valley with some dear friends of ours. At the time, I didn't realize that this would be a baptism by grape juice. My friend Tim was on a mission to make us learn, drink, and fall in love with fantastic wine.

We came home from that trip loving wine. Truly. After all, what's not to love? It's a drink that can be enjoyed with any occasion in life. We celebrate with wine. We mourn with wine. We Tuesday with wine. There is a wine for every time, place, food, occasion, and friend. Wine was once used for medicinal purposes. Wine was used to sterilize water. Wine was the focus of Jesus' first miracle. Some wines are simply miraculous. It's the most popular beverage in the world, and for good cause! So why is it that so many people find wine so intimidating?

Wine has a bit of an image problem for a lot of consumers. It seems a little too sophisticated, and that can be a turnoff. There is also a vast ocean of wines to explore at a broad spectrum of prices. Regardless of what you've heard, your odds of finding a remarkable bottle go up as the price goes up. That's not to say that all low-cost wine is bad or all high-cost wine is good. There is great wine to be found at all price points, but where do you start looking for the needle, and how big is the haystack?

This chapter isn't intended to answer all of your questions about wine. You will, however, get a brief overview of what happens in the vineyard and the importance this plays in winemaking. You will also get some insights into what happens in the winery to make grapes into wine. Lastly, you will explore a handful of the top red and white wine-making grape varietals, the nuances of the resulting wines, and how those wines can pair with food.

Making Wine

Fermented beverages all follow the same general process: A liquid mixture containing a sugar is inoculated with yeast. The yeast comes alive and starts eating the sugar. As the yeast consumes the sugar, it produces carbon dioxide and alcohol. This process continues until all of the fermentable sugar is consumed or enough alcohol is made that the environment becomes toxic to the yeast and the yeast begins to die off. This is a very rudimentary description of the production of alcohol; the actual process is much more refined and scientific. It has to be to produce high-quality drinks. In Chapter 3, I talk about how important high-quality ingredients are to making high-quality charcuterie; the same goes for wine making!

Great wines start in the vineyard with the production of great grapes. Then the high-quality fruit is processed to make high-quality wine. There are a lot of factors that go into both parts of this process!

In the vineyard

Growing good grapes is no small task! Grapes can grow pretty much anywhere in the world where there are decent growing conditions. You can grow grapes in dry climates and hot, humid climates. But growing grapes for making wine requires a very particular blend of environmental variables. The French word *terroir* is meant to encapsulate all of these variables, which include soil, topography, and climate. Good terroir is necessary for growing good grapes. However, good terroir is also not what you might think! To grow large, healthy, nutritious fruits and vegetables, generally speaking, you want fertile soil, plenty of rain, and a lot of sun. To grow exceptional wine grapes, you want almost the opposite.

Grapes grown in moist, fertile soil grow big berries filled with juice. However, they also lack a concentration of flavor, and the resulting wines are generally bland, lacking in structure, and not enjoyable. On the contrary, grape vines that struggle tend to have incredibly concentrated flavor in the berries. Sounds backwards, doesn't it? I'll say it again: the vine that struggles a lot, produces better fruit than the vine that doesn't struggle at all. Look at some of the most well-known wine regions; generally speaking, they aren't fertile plains. To further complicate things, each variety of wine grape prefers a very precise set of environmental variables. Making great wines means growing the right grape. For example, when you think of great American Cabernet, you might think Napa and not Oregon. Figure 9-1 is a picture of the northern part of the Napa Valley.

FIGURE 9-1:
Napa Valley.

Mark LaFay

To produce great grapes, the grape grower has to pay a lot of attention to the vines throughout the growing season to ensure they are ripening at the correct rate. Timing is everything. If the grapes don't ripen enough by the time the season is coming to an end, the resulting wines will be bitter, astringent, and "green" tasting — think bell pepper. If the grapes ripen too quickly, they could have a high sugar content and low acidity, resulting in wines with high alcohol and no character. Thankfully, grape growers have some tools that enable them to manage environmental variables. They can control sun exposure by how they orient their vines in the vineyard at planting. They can control shade on the berries by how they train the vines and manage the canopy of leaves. They can use irrigation if there isn't enough rain. Growers can even drop green fruit so the vines have fewer clusters of fruit to ripen.

One thing that growers can't control, however, is the weather. Some years can just be difficult years to grow because the weather doesn't play nice. This is the largest factor that differentiates wines from vintage to vintage, and it takes a wine maker with a deft hand to be able to produce a consistently good wine despite the year's growing conditions! The cost of a wine is greatly impacted by the cost of the land where the grapes are produced, the yield per acre of land, and the intangible factors of name, brand, and place.

In the winery

Once the grapes are harvested, they go to the winery to get turned into wine. The steps in this process are generally the same, but the way in which these steps are performed is what separates a high-quality wine from a low-quality wine. Here are the basic steps:

1. Grapes are delivered to the winery and sorted.

2. The grapes are crushed and dumped into vats. The juice settles and the non-liquid grape material floats to the top (this is called a *cap*).

3. Yeast is introduced (either by physically adding a starter culture, or by allowing natural yeasts to do it on their own).

4. Once fermentation is complete, the juice is pressed or drained off.

5. The wine is filtered.

6. The filtered wine is aged in concrete, steel, or wood vats, or in barrels.

7. The wine is bottled.

This is a very high-level explanation of the process. In general, the larger the operation, the less meticulous it is in terms of quality, and the more emphasis is placed on efficiency and consistency. Thus you get a cheaper, lower-quality product. The smaller the operation, the more manual it may be and the more care is put into it. This also means higher costs. Figure 9-2 is a picture of a the production facility of the Montes Winery in the Apalta region of the Colchagua Valley in Chile.

In a smaller, higher-quality producer's winery, much more attention is given to each step of the process. This starts with how the grapes are harvested and follows through every step to bottling and cellaring. Here is the process a high-quality producer may follow when producing a premium wine:

FIGURE 9-2:
Montes production facility.

Mark LaFay

1. Grapes are hand-harvested and delivered to the winery. Once at the winery, they are put onto a sorting conveyer with dry ice to cool them down. Sorting is done manually as the grapes move down the line. Green grapes, under-ripe grapes, and materials other than grapes (*mog*) are all removed.

2. The grapes are de-stemmed. Stems can impart extra tannin and sometimes a "green" herbal or medicinal quality to the wine. Leaving in or removing the stem is done at the wine maker's discretion.

3. The berries are gently pressed using a bladder press. A bladder press extracts juice from berries by inflating a bladder with air or water; as it inflates, the bladder presses the berries against the sides of the cylinder.

4. The juice settles to the bottom of the tank, and the skins and grape material float to the top, creating a cap. The cap can then be punched down manually to maximize contact with the juice and increase extraction of flavor, color, and tannin. Tannin is a biochemical found in the skin and the stems of the grapes. It imparts bitterness, astringency, and complexity. It also has a preserving quality.

5. After fermentation and aging, the juice is drained and separated from the cap. It is then filtered and put into oak barrels to age. Several different types of oak barrels may be employed, some brand new, some used. Some barrels may have a light toast (lightly burned on the inside), and others a medium toast. Figure 9-3 is a picture of the barrels stacked up in the Bennett Lane winery

FIGURE 9-3:
Barrels in a cellar.

Mark LaFay

6. The wine is left to age for 10 to 16 months before it is clarified and then bottled.

7. After bottling, the wine is left to age in the cellar until the wine maker believes it is ready for release.

Again, this is still a very basic overview of the process, but as you can see, it is more labor intensive, takes more time, and has a great level of finesse involved. Wines made with this level of care can reach a far higher quality than wines made on an industrial scale. Combine this level of care with high-quality fruits and you have a potential recipe for something truly great.

Red Wines

At a very generic level, wine can be grouped into two primary categories: red and white. This designation has to do with the color of the wine in the bottle, but did you know that grape juice actually contains no color whatsoever? Grape juice is clear; the color actually comes from the skin of the berry. When wine is pressed, the juice runs clear. The longer the juice is soaked on the skins, the more color is extracted. In addition to color, the skin of red grapes contains the following components.

>> **Tannin:** Tannin is an organic chemical compound found in plant material. Specific to grapes, tannin is found in the stems, seeds, and skin of the grape berry. Tannin imparts bitterness and astringency, which is the "drying" feeling you get on your tongue when you drink dry, red wine that contains high quantities of tannin. Tannin can also be imparted in wine by contact with oak.

>> **Aroma:** Several biochemicals in the skin of the grape play a role in the smells of the wine in a glass.

>> **Yeast:** Yeast cells are microorganisms that exist everywhere. Yeasts produce all sorts of by-products as they feed and replicate. Wild yeast is often deposited by the wind onto the skins of grapes. When the grapes come into the winery, they are crushed, and that yeast "activates" in the juice and begins the fermentation process. This is often referred to as *natural fermentation*.

Red wines can be greatly nuanced, very robust, and full of flavor and punch, depending on the grape variety, cultivation, and methods used in the winery. Generally speaking, when drinking red wines, you will smell and taste red, blue, and black fruit flavors. Examples include the following.

>> **Red fruits:** cherry, raspberry, strawberry, currant, pomegranate, and cranberry.

>> **Black fruits:** plum, prune, black cherry, black raspberry, and blackberry.

>> **Blue fruit:** blueberry.

In addition to fruit flavors, red grapes can have aromas and flavors of various herbs, spices, and floral characteristics, all of which are a result of the grape variety, growing location, growing conditions, soil type, and production methods in the winery. These flavors can dull over time, creating room for secondary and even tertiary flavors, depending on how long and well the bottle is aged. Most wines are meant to be drunk "young" and their vibrancy enjoyed. There are also wines, primarily very premium wines, that require age to be truly enjoyed. To put it simply, aging a wine is allowing it to slowly be affected by trace amounts of oxygen, which either exist in the bottle or access the bottle through an organic cork. This oxidation will mellow out tannins, soften big stand-out flavors, and make them blend together, giving way to secondary flavors.

For the most part, oxygen contact with the wine must be controlled during the wine-making process so that the wine doesn't oxidize and spoil. For you, the wine drinker, oxygen is what "wakes up" the wine. Red wines are poured into larger glasses so that the wine can have greater contact with oxygen. The oxygen will react with the wine in the glass to bring out the flavors. It sounds crazy, right? But try a little experiment: Open a bottle of red wine and pour two glasses. Taste the first glass right away and write down what you tasted. Wait 1 to 2 hours and taste the other glass of wine. You'll probably notice that the two experiences are vastly different.

Each grape brings something different to the glass, and while there are thousands of red grape varieties, here I'll talk about the five most popular red varieties and how you can pair wines made from these grapes with delicious foods!

Cabernet Sauvignon

The world's most popular grape is Cabernet Sauvignon. This grape is a natural cross between Cabernet Franc and Sauvignon Blanc, which are a red and white grape, respectively. Depending on where it is grown, Cabernet Sauvignon can be very fruit-forward or it can be very savory and earthy. Cabernet Sauvignon–based wines are full bodied and have higher amounts of tannin, which often gives them a drier flavor and texture. The grape tends to showcase darker fruit flavors like blackberry, black cherry, and black currant. Spices and mineral flavors like black licorice, pipe tobacco, baking spices (often the result of oak aging), mint, slate, and graphite are all possibilities as well!

World-class Cabernet Sauvignon wine is produced in numerous regions around the globe, each with its own nuance affecting the grape and wine. Three of these regions are detailed here.

>> **France:** The Bordeaux region is responsible for the bulk of Cabernet Sauvignon–based wines in France. France has been making wines from this grape (and several others) for the longest. Wines made with Cabernet are bold, but not too big. They are dry and tannic, and the acidity of these wines can be on the high end of moderate. French Cabernet is big and bold, but more reserved than Cabernet wines from the United States.

>> **America:** Cabernet Sauvignon wines are made all over the west coast of the United States. The most famous wine region is Napa Valley, and the more premium wines come from this area. Central Valley is responsible for the bulk jug-wine production that you should avoid. Great Cabernet can also be found on the north coast of California, and Washington State is producing great Cabernet wines as well. The American Cabernets are generally high in alcohol and very extracted, and they get a lot of oak treatment. American wines, not just cabernet, can have higher residual sugar that is masked by alcohol, grape, and oak tannin. Generally speaking, American Cabernet is fruit-forward and meant to be consumed young.

>> **Chile:** The Maipo and Colchagua Valleys in Chile are responsible for the production of fantastic Cabernet-based wines. Cabernet-based wines from this region are similar to American Cabernet, but not as bold and extracted. These wines are fruit-forward and delicious but are not nearly as big. Chile presents the greatest "bang for the buck" with their wines as well, and so you can get great wine at even better prices.

Cabernet pairs well with cheeses like aged cheddar, Gruyère, and Gouda. Salamis, both spicy and mild, pair nicely with Cabernet-based wines as well.

Pinot Noir

Pinot Noir is the grape responsible for some of the most expensive and sought-after wines in the world. Wines made from Pinot Noir are medium-body wines that generally have high acidity. The grape thrives in cooler climates where it can slowly ripen over the growing season. Pinot Noir wines showcase red fruits like red cherries and raspberries, with secondary flavors like tea, rose, and damp leaves. Location and production methods have a major effect on this particular grape. It is very finicky and requires a lot more effort in the vineyard to produce quality crops. Two regions of the world are known for exceptional Pinot Noir production: France and America.

» **France:** Shocking to hear that France makes great Pinot Noir wines, right? They are the originators of a lot of wine culture today. The Burgundy region is known for legendary Pinot Noir, which has been grown there for a few hundred years. Pinot here is higher in acidity and has a pronounced mineral profile, and while there are many red cherry and floral characteristics on the nose, there are also wet forest, wet leaves, and other organic components on the palate.

» **America:** In the past 30 years, wine making in Oregon has really grown and developed. The primary grape grown in Oregon is Pinot Noir. The cool climate is similar to that found in Burgundy, and the region itself sits on the same latitude as the southern part of Burgundy (Beaujolais). Pinot Noir made in Oregon is very fruit-forward on the nose and palate. Flavors of red cherry and raspberry are prominent. Earth flavors (dirt, not wet forest) are also prominent. The Central Coast of California is also home to some world-class Pinot. The California style is vastly different from that of Oregon. The fruit is a little more ripe, the wine style is a little bolder, and the alcohol content can be a little higher.

Pinot Noir pairs very nicely with many cheeses, including Brie, Gouda, Comté, and Gruyère, but try to stay away from very acidic cheeses, like goat cheese. Pinot Noir also pairs nicely with prosciutto, coppa, and fatty pâtés.

Merlot

Merlot is a delightful wine that got a bit of a bad reputation in the 1990s, maybe because of a movie called *Sideways*, and maybe because a lot of bad Merlot was being made in the U.S. There is also a lot of good Merlot. Merlot is grown all over the world, and you can find great wines made from Merlot in most regions. Merlots are generally very dry, full-bodied wines with a good deal of tannin. In France, Merlot is a great blending varietal with Cabernet Sauvignon and Cabernet Franc. Merlot offers a great fruit profile, with red cherry and sometimes dark cherries as well. Merlot wines take oak treatment very well and often receive a lot of it, which imparts baking spices and vanilla. Several regions produce Merlot, including the following.

>> **France:** You betcha, France again. Merlot is generally included in Bordeaux blends which also include Cabernet Sauvignon, Cabernet Franc, Petite Verdot, and Malbec. Bordeaux has a moderate to cool climate, which makes Merlot from this area a little more tart, with red cherry and raspberry but also some darker, spicy notes like black licorice.

>> **America:** Merlot is generally grown in Napa Valley, where it is warm and dry. Merlot wines made in Napa are bolder, show more fresh fruit, and have more red cherry, black cherry, and even blackberry. These wines are higher in alcohol, more extracted, and darker in color. They also receive much more oak during the aging process, which imparts baking spices and vanilla. Napa Merlot and Australian Merlot have a lot in common, although you may find more "green" or "leafy" characteristics in Australian Merlot.

TIP

Merlot pairs well with several cheeses like Brie, Camembert, Gorgonzola, Stilton, Gouda, aged Parmesan, aged cheddar, and aged pecorino. Pair Merlot with hard salamis that don't have big spice profiles.

Syrah

Syrah is a powerhouse wine that doesn't necessarily have the same amount of tannin as Cabernet and Merlot, but it has a very full body. It's a chewy, meaty wine with a lot of black cherry, blackberry, blueberry, plum, prune, black licorice, pipe tobacco, and other full, rich flavors. This grape has a moderate amount of acidity, and the flavor profile, like most grapes, is largely influenced by the location and method with which it is produced. Syrah is grown globally, but most of it is produced in two countries: France and Australia.

>> **France:** The bulk of Syrah production in France happens in the Rhône Valley. The most revered Syrah comes from Hermitage and Côte-Rôtie. Syrah from these areas has slightly higher acidity than Syrah from other regions of the world. French Syrah has copious black fruit, pepper, earth, and organic characteristics. It is also used for blending in a big, bold French wine called Châteauneuf-du-Pape.

TIP

Syrah is a spicy, bold grape that pairs wonderfully with smokey and spicy foods. Surprise yourself and drink it with barbecue or Indian food. Syrah pairs nicely with cheddar, Gouda (try the cheap, smoked Gouda found in the U.S.), and Parmesan. Syrah pairs nicely with speck (smoked prosciutto), smoked beef sticks, and summer sausage.

Sangiovese

The name *Sangiovese* is derived from the Latin words for "blood of Jove." This grape is the pride of Italy and the dominant grape of the Tuscany and Umbria regions. Sangiovese is grown in small amounts in other parts of the world, but there is no point talking about them. Seriously, the best representation of the Sangiovese grape is that which is grown in the Tuscan hillsides! Sangiovese is the primary grape of Chianti, Chianti Classico, Chianti Classico Reserva, Brunello di Montalcino, Rosso di Montalcino, and several other wines. These wines are all protected by law in Italy and are only made in their respective pockets of the Tuscany wine-making region!

Take a trip through Tuscany and get dinner. The house wine is almost always a Sangiovese-based wine. In the case of Chianti, Chianti Classico, and Chianti Classico Reserva, the Sangiovese that is grown and used is medium-bodied with slightly elevated acidity and moderate tannins. The wines have bright-red cherry on the nose and on the palate, but mixed in you will find an organic funk that is indicative of Italian wines. You will also taste roasted tomatoes, and maybe some balsamic. For a more refined and assertive version of Sangiovese, look to the hills surrounding the town of Montalcino for Brunello di Montalcino.

TIP

Sangiovese is a versatile wine that can be paired with steak or pasta. It is great with Parmesan, pecorino, provolone, mozzarella, Stilton, and other blue cheeses. It also goes well with all sorts of cured meats, both whole-muscle and salami.

White Wines

White wines are often regarded as the wines of spring and summertime. They are often light, refreshing, and served slightly chilled. For these reasons, they tend to be better suited to a warm, sunny day. I enjoy white wine nearly year-round.

Much like red wine, thousands of white wine grapes are found all over the world, each with their own genetic characteristics that make them unique. There are, however, a select few that are cultivated for commercial wine growing. The process for making white wine is very similar to the process for making red wine. White wines, however, are more delicate than reds, and so they require some special handling in the winery.

White wines lack pigment in the grape skins, and pigment provides tannic structure to a wine. That means that white wines are naturally very low in tannin. However, they can have bitterness that is imparted by phenolic compounds in the skin; in some wines the bitterness can be detected, but for the most part, it is not discernable and simply helps give structure to the wines.

White wines have lighter fruit flavors that can be grouped into the following categories.

>> **Stone fruit:** peaches, nectarines, apricots, and lychees.

>> **Apples and pears:** yellow apples, green apples, red apples, Bosc pears, Bartlett pears, and Anjou pears.

>> **Citrus:** lemon, lime, grapefruit, orange, and tangerine.

White wines can also have a great deal of nonfruit characteristics that are just as intriguing as, if not more intriguing than, the fruit flavors. Floral characteristics can really shine through in white wines; white and light-colored flowers come to mind with many of these wines. Spices and herbs can shine through as well. If the white wine is aged in oak barrels, then you can find baking spice, vanilla, and some "butter" notes. White wines often also go through a secondary fermentation called *malolactic fermentation*. In this process, an additional yeast strain is added to the wine after alcoholic fermentation, and converts the malic acid in the wine to lactic acid. This process has a "rounding" effect on the wine; it smooths it out by replacing the harsher malic acid with lactic acid. This can also impart a creaminess to the wine.

Because white wines lack the tannic structure of red wines, acidity becomes even more important to the wine. White grapes need to be higher in acid to create bright, vibrant white wines. The mineral profile of a white wine is also critical. Different minerals are introduced to wines through soils. White wines tend to show off minerals more than red wines. Sometimes minerals will shine through in a white wine and almost seem like acidity because of the way they tickle the tongue when you drink them. Components of soil can usually be picked out by a trained palate.

The moral of the story is that white wines are just as unique, complex, and interesting as red wines. They have their own nuances that make them very enjoyable, and even if you aren't a "white-wine person," you should explore the world of white wines! Keep reading to learn about the nuances of the four most popular white grapes.

Chardonnay

The world's most widely planted grape is, you guessed it, Chardonnay! Chardonnay grapes can be found in most of the wine-growing regions of the world. They have a tendency to really pick up characteristics of the soil and carry them through into the wine. For that reason, Chardonnay tastes wildly different, depending on where it is grown.

Burgundy is widely regarded as the birthplace of Chardonnay. Here you will find a very pure, refined version of Chardonnay, and many Chardonnays from Burgundy are so structured that they can age for decades. Not all Chardonnay is meant to be consumed with age, though. In fact, fresh Chardonnay is quite delightful, which is a big reason why it is so loved around the world. Chardonnay can have flavors of lemon citrus, lemon peel, yellow apples, pears, and even tropical fruits like pineapple and star fruit. Chardonnay that is not aged in oak tends to have a crisper texture, and to show more fruit, earth, and minerals. Oaked Chardonnay has a rounder texture; the fruit profile often feels more ripe, and the baking spices, vanilla, and "butter" will be ever-present, depending on the amount of new oak used to ferment and age the wine. Several wine regions produce Chardonnay, but the following are the two most dominant.

>> **France:** Burgundy, which is the home of world-class Pinot Noir, is also the home of legendary Chardonnay. The region has ideal conditions for producing Chardonnay that is sharp, crisp, and full of flavor. These wines are generally fermented and aged in either steel or concrete vats, so "butter" and baking spices are rarely found in these wines. Some wine producers will use full or partial malolactic fermentation to round out the wines, but this is a preference, not a requirement.

>> **America:** Much of the Chardonnay in America comes from California. The Central Coast, North Coast, and Sonoma County produce quite a bit of Chardonnay. The temperature is warmer than in Burgundy and often sunnier, so the fruit gets ripe faster. Chardonnay has a firm foothold in Oregon as well. The wine-making styles in Oregon and California are very different because of climate differences. California Chardonnays tend to be larger in body, round, fruit-forward, and often buttery from oak treatment, though not always. Chardonnays from Oregon tend to be leaner, fruit-forward, and have a more pronounced acid backbone.

TIP

Chardonnay is a very versatile wine that can be paired with a great number of cheeses, like Brie, Camembert, Stilton, Parmesan, Gouda, and Gruyère. Chardonnay also pairs nicely with pâté, salamis, whole muscle like prosciutto, and other meats that do not have "hot" spices.

Riesling

In my experience as first a wine drinker and second as a certified sommelier, Riesling is one of the more polarizing wines of the world. For a lot of Americans, when you hear the word "Riesling," you think of a blue bottle filled with a cloying, sweet liquid that is not particularly appealing. Truth be told, Riesling is probably my favorite white wine varietal. There are several different types of Riesling, and the wine is made on a sweetness spectrum ranging from bone dry to very sweet. The sweeter versions tend to be lower in alcohol and extremely age-worthy. The dry versions can be very age-worthy as well, but are ideally consumed younger.

Riesling is a very fruit-forward wine. The fruit profile is usually so prominent that the fruit flavors can lead one to believe the wine has elevated residual sugar when in actuality it is bone dry. Similar to Chardonnay, Riesling shows off the soil where it is grown. For that reason, a trained palate can easily differentiate between Rieslings from Alsace, Rheingau, Mosel, and other regions of the world. Riesling has a very diverse range of possible fruit flavors, including lime, lemon, peach, apricot, apple, pear, and pineapple. Typical aromas include honey, beeswax, ginger, citrus blossom, rubber, and petrol. Excellent Riesling is being produced in Washington, Oregon, and Australia, and you should note that the Traverse City area of Michigan is starting to produce some stellar Riesling as well! However, the two big, bad daddy regions for Riesling are listed here.

>> **France:** Alsace, France, is a wine region just to the east of the Vosges mountain range. This region is the northernmost wine region in Europe, which, as you can imagine, means it is cold. It is also a dry area because it sits in the rain shadow of the mountain range. Riesling from this area tends to be quite powerful, mineral rich, floral, and peachy. Drink it dry; drink it often!

>> **Germany:** The two main areas for Riesling production are the Rheingau and the Mosel, and each one offers a distinct difference in their Rieslings. Rieslings from Rheingau are lower in acid and have peach and spicy lime flavors, whereas Mosel Rieslings have much higher acidity, as well as citrus. The minerals of Mosel Riesling tend to really pop because of the soil, which is packed full of slate.

TIP

Rieslings are fantastic wines that can pair with a whole slew of different foods. Dry Rieslings in particular are where you should focus your attention. Do not try to pair them with stinky cheese. Stick to Blue, Brie, Gouda, and mild cheddar. You can also drink dry Riesling with spicy salami.

Sauvignon Blanc

Sauvignon blanc is one of the parent grapes of Cabernet Sauvignon. It is a delicious grape that can have all sorts of pungent aromas. The power of suggestion can lead you toward grapefruit skin, peach skin, fresh-cut grass, or something more feral. Sauvignon blanc is often much more herbaceous, and it is always bone dry. A great deal of Sauvignon blanc is made all over the world, and each location introduces some pretty interesting characteristics that can be discerned without too much work. Are you starting to see a trend in how terroir affects wine? Flavors like lime, green apple, guava, and white peach are all very common for Sauvignon blanc. Aromas like green bell pepper, jalapeno, grass, lemon grass, and wet concrete are common as well. Sauvignon blanc is grown in several regions around the world, including the following three.

>> **France:** The Loire Valley is a wine-growing region in France that follows the Loire River as it moves west toward the Atlantic Ocean. There are numerous small wine-growing regions within the Loire Valley that specialize in different wines. Sancerre is one of these regions, and their specialty is Sauvignon blanc. Sauvignon blanc from Sancerre is often high in acid, and bright with lime, peach, and peach skin; it also has a pronounced mineral profile. Let the record reflect that this is my favorite Sauvignon blanc wine.

>> **New Zealand:** There are over 41,000 acres of Sauvignon blanc in New Zealand across several smaller wine-growing areas. Marlborough is probably the most esteemed region among them. Sauvignon blanc from Marlborough has a very pronounced grapefruit aroma that can border on the taste of cut grass. In fact, the grassy characteristic is usually a dead giveaway of its origin. The Marlboroughs are delicious and unique wines.

>> **America:** Sauvignon blanc made in California is generally riper, rounder, and more fruit-forward. It doesn't have the grassy nature of New Zealand Sauvignon blanc. It also lacks the flinty, mineral-forward nature of Sancerre. The California variety is easy to approach and has broader appeal to Americans. The acid content is lower, giving way to a smoother experience. I would contend that California Sauvignon blanc, while still very different, is closer to Chardonnay than Sauvignon blanc from anywhere else in the world.

TIP

Sauvignon blanc can have a very diverse range of flavors depending on the region where it is produced. However, regardless of its origins, you can pair Sauvignon blanc with goat cheese, Saint-André, and Gruyère. Pairing Sauvignon blanc with salamis can be tricky, so try lower-salt salamis without big spice profiles.

Pinot Grigio / Pinot Gris

Did you know that Pinot Grigio and Pinot Gris are the same thing? Surprise! This grape is sort of a weird one. It is a genetic mutation of Pinot Noir with a slightly grayish-red skin (yes, it is a white wine), and it can take on some pretty unique characteristics! For years, Pinot Grigio has received a bad reputation because a version of it is mass produced, almost flavorless, and exported in tanker loads to the United States. There is also a Pinot Grigio that is rich, vibrant, and truly memorable! Let's talk about that one. This grape is responsible for wines that can have flavors of lime, green apple, lemon, and nectarine. Other notes of white flowers, bitter almond, and almost saline minerality are present in higher-quality Pinot Gris! Pinot Grigio / Gris is made in several regions around the globe; following are two of the best.

>> **Italy:** Pinot Grigio generally refers to Pinot Gris made in Italy. A bunch of low-quality Grigio is made in Italy. For the higher-quality stuff, you need to look to the region of Trentino–Alto Adige. This area is as much Austrian as it is Italian. It sits in the foothills of the Alps and has a relatively cool climate. Pinot Grigio made in this region is mineral-forward and vibrant!

>> **France:** Pinot Gris is at its best when it comes from Alsace. The home of killer Riesling is also home to outstanding Pinot Gris. Pinot Gris from Alsace tends to have more fruit characteristics and slightly honeyed notes to complement a firm mineral profile.

TIP

Pinot Grigio / Gris is a versatile white wine that can be a star or a supporting actress, depending on where it originates. Pair with mozzarella, Gruyère, baby Swiss, or goat cheese. Also enjoy with prosciutto, coppa, or culatello.

Chapter **10**

Beer and Charcuterie

Beer is proof God loves us and wants us to be happy.
— (LIKELY NOT) BENJAMIN FRANKLIN

G rowing up, I remember seeing different types of beer commercials that would portray people working hard or partying hard. Typically the commercials were for the big beer brands like Budweiser, Miller, Coors, Michelob, Rolling Rock, and . . . you get the idea. Beer was beer flavored and it was generally considered a very accessible adult beverage. That is to say, it didn't have the prestige, pretense, or sophistication of wine or fancy booze. Growing up, my dad taught us that beer wasn't a race to the finish. You had to drink it slowly. Looking back, I now realize that was less about savoring the flavor and more about elongating your sober consumption; words of wisdom, nonetheless.

Today, American awareness of global beer styles has grown substantially from when I was a kid. Interest in traditional beer styles, plus the growing enthusiasm for supporting local business, has fueled the growth of local breweries. The growing concentration of craft breweries all vying for the same consumer dollars has driven a lot of innovation in flavors and styles of beer. In the last 10 to 15 years, beer has even become culinary in a sense. Beers have all sorts of non-typical ingredients that impart all sorts of flavors to what would be typical styles of beer. Beer is no longer just for quenching thirst at the end of a long day; it's for sipping, pontificating, and pairing with food. While some big beer companies say that it shouldn't be fussed over, many beer lovers feel differently!

In this chapter you will explore the fundamentals of making beer. Part of this exploration will include a brief overview of the different ingredients in beer and the part they play in giving beer its unique flavors. You will learn about several different beer styles and get a brief introduction to a few commercial beers of each style. Last but not least, you'll get a sense of how different beers can actually be paired with different meats and cheeses.

Making Beer

If you want to learn how to make beer, watch a Coors Light commercial and you'll have it all figured out. Okay, maybe not. But the process of making beer is very similar in theory to the process of making any other fermented beverage. Water and some sort of fermentable sugar and yeast are the core components. The yeast wakes up in the water and starts eating the fermentable sugars. As the yeast eats the sugars, it produces carbon dioxide and alcohol. For wine, grape juice contains water and fermentable sugars, and the yeast turns the juice into wine. Beer, however is a combination of water, grain, yeast, and hops. The following is a very rudimentary outline of the process of making beer.

1. *Grist* (ground grains) is mixed with water and heated. This breaks down the grains' starch into sugars through a natural enzymatic process. This mixture is referred to as the *mash*.

2. The liquid is poured off the mash. This liquid, which contains the sugars, is called the *wort*.

3. The wort is collected in a kettle that is brought to a boil. At this point, the hops are added.

4. After the boil, the wort is cooled and transferred to a fermentation vessel.

5. Yeast is added to the cooled wort to start fermentation.

6. Once fermentation is complete, the beer is poured off and in some cases filtered.

7. The beer is given time to mature before carbonation and bottling.

This is a very brief overview of the process of beer making, but as you probably noticed, there are a lot of ways that the flavor of the beer can be influenced throughout the process. Without getting too far into the weeds, take a look at the following four key ingredients.

» **Water:** Water is one of the main ingredients in beer, and its impact on flavor cannot be overlooked. Water can be completely neutral, or it can contain a great deal of dissolved solids. Whatever is dissolved in water will impart a flavor to the water. Water profiles can be largely impacted by geography; however, breweries can now impart any taste to their water by stripping everything from the water through reverse osmosis and then adding different minerals in trace amounts.

» **Grains:** The choice of grains used in classic beers was largely a result of availability. If you had a lot of wheat around, you would make beer with wheat, if you had rice, you used rice, and so on. There are several different types of grains that can be used in beer making, all of which impart different characteristics. Generally speaking, beer is made with barley, and then additional grains like rice, corn, wheat, rye, oats, and so on can be introduced to add nuance to the beer.

» **Yeast:** These little microorganisms exist everywhere in the world. There are wild yeasts that differ from place to place, and there are also cultivated yeasts. Both wild and cultivated yeasts can be used in beer making, but every strain of yeast imparts something slightly different. Wild yeasts can impart funky, almost barnyard-like flavors, and are more commonly found in farmhouse-style ales and sours. Cultivated yeasts give the brewer more control and consistency because the yeasts are isolated and their characteristics are documented.

» **Hops:** To manage the sweetness of beer and to impart floral, herbal, medicinal, and fruit flavors, brewers add hops to the beer. Hops are the flower, or cone, of the *Humulus lupulus* plant, and their first documented introduction to beer dates back to 900 A.D. Hops impart bitterness and have a slight antibacterial effect on the beer. They provide balance to beer, although today over-hopping to make beer extra bitter is generally the norm.

Each ingredient can be nuanced to create uniqueness in a beer. In addition to these core ingredients, the brewer can also add other ingredients at different phases to impart flavor. Fruit additions, chocolate, coffee, herbs, spices, fruit rinds, and so on can be used with different beer styles to produce desirable characteristics. Beers can also be aged in oak barrels to impart some of the flavors of the wood, much the same as in wine making. Aging beer in barrels, a technique once used for aging wine or spirits, can add even more unique nuances to the beer.

Popular Beer Styles

There is no universally agreed-upon list of beer styles, but the Beer Judge Certification Program categorizes beer into 26 master styles and 85 sub-styles, along with several historical variations. So let's say all beer in the world can be grouped into 85 styles; that's a lot of styles! Within those 85 styles of beer, there are thousands of different beers that showcase the preference and personality of the brewer. Navigating beer is almost as daunting a task as for wine. Also, the more exotic the ingredients or process involved in making the beer, the more expensive it is. As a result, guessing your way through a beer flight can be a costly adventure or mishap! In the following section, you will find a list of the six most globally popular styles (big "S" styles) of beer.

Standard American beer

The Germans didn't invent beer, but it can be argued that they perfected it. German immigrants to America brought their history, experience, and traditions with them, and thankfully, part of that was beer making. Beer was (and still is) big business in America, but both Prohibition and World War II spurred a lot of consolidation within the American beer industry. With consolidation came a desire to appeal to larger swaths of people, and so American lager evolved to become slightly more bland, but more widely loved. That isn't to say that standard American lagers are bland, but they can be and many are.

Standard American-style beers are refreshing, easy to drink, and perfect bedfellows with salty snacks. Following are some examples of standard American beers.

>> **Coors Banquet:** Tap the Rockies for this delicious American lager. The Coors Brewing Company was brewing beers in Colorado before Colorado was a state, and their history really is worth a read if you ever get the time. Coors Banquet was the flagship beer of the company. This beer is light-bodied, crisp, very refreshing, and dry with a slight, sweet finish.

>> **Prima Pils:** Victory Brewing Company is located in Downingtown, Pennsylvania. Founded in 1996, they are a craft brewery with several different flagship beers that are distributed in 34 states. The Prima Pils is a German-style pilsner made with plenty of whole German and Czech hops. This beer has more body than Coors and a far more present hop profile than the typical standard American lager.

>> **Champagne Velvet:** Upland Brewing Company was founded in 1997 in the town of Bloomington, home of Indiana University. They have grown steadily since then and currently produce several different beers. In 2012, Upland

acquired the rights to Champagne Velvet, a pre-Prohibition pilsner that was originally made by the Terre Haute Brewing Company in 1902! Not many pre-Prohibition–style beers are commercially made anymore. Champagne Velvet has the light body of a pilsner with a latent sweetness that comes from the small amount of corn that is used.

TIP

All of these beers are easy-to-drink, delightful beverages that are refreshing and appealing to a large base of beer drinkers. Pair these beers with milder cheeses like mozzarella, Gouda, and mild cheddar. They also pair nicely with salt-cured meats. Their mild nature makes them a great accompaniment with mild and spicy salamis.

Wheat beer

Beers with a grain bill of which wheat makes up a substantial portion are generally referred to as *wheat beers*. Wheat beers are tougher to brew because the starches and the proteins in the wheat want to stick together, making it harder to extract the sugars. (Sugars are necessary for fermenting.) There are several types of wheat beers. The German varieties generally need to be at least 50-percent wheat, whereas the American wheat beers are 10- to 35-percent wheat. Wheat gives beer a creamier texture, and these beers are generally hazy because of the increased amount of suspended proteins. The flavor is bready, has hints of citrus, and in the case of German beers, can have a banana-and-clove thing going on. Following are some popular wheat beers that you'll want to try if you haven't already.

>> **Oberon:** Bell's Brewery is a craft brewery that was founded in Kalamazoo, Michigan. Larry Bell marketed his first commercial beer in 1985, and, my oh my, have things changed since then. If you get a chance to visit the taproom, do it; great food and beer are plentiful. Bell's Oberon is a seasonal American wheat ale that is light and delicious. It has a spicy, orange flavor and is summer in bottle form.

>> **Franziskaner:** As you may have guessed, Spaten-Franziskaner-Bräu is a German brewery. They're also one of the older breweries in the world, and are believed to have started around 1397. Franziskaner is the archetype German wheat beer. It is cloudy, smooth, and has flavors of banana and clove, as well as hints of vanilla and spice. Try this one, and then try other wheat beers.

>> **Blue Moon:** Blue Moon was created at the Sandlot Brewery at Coors Field in Denver, which also used to be the only place you could get it. Well. Its popularity led to it being purchased by MillerCoors, and now it can be found almost anywhere in the world. The beer is a Belgian-inspired white wheat beer. It is brewed with coriander and orange peel, both of which carry through to the glass. This beer is refreshing and smooth.

Numerous wheat beers are in production all over the U.S. by a variety of craft breweries. The German renditions are the original ones, so definitely do some exploring there as well. These beers are light, sweeter on the palate, and usually have some sort of tropical fruit-and-spice component.

TIP

Try pairing wheat beers with acidic cheeses like goat or Manchego. You can also pair them with creamy cheeses like Brie, Camembert, or Saint-André.

Belgian ales

Belgian beers are a mystical and wonderful thing. They are not like any other beer in the world, and it is almost impossible to replicate a Belgian ale if you are not brewing it in Belgium. It may be the cross-pollination of the beer-drinking culture of the Germans combined with the wine-drinking culture of the French. Whatever it is, the Belgians nailed it. There are several styles of Belgian ales, but I won't get too far into the weeds on that. Belgian beers have included Trappist ales (made in monasteries), sours, wheat beers (witbiers), farmhouse ales, and more. One commonality among all of them is that the yeast gives all Belgian beers a barnyard flavor to some extent. Wild yeasts like Brettanomyces impart a grassy, hay-like, spicy flavor to the beers. Saison, witbier, lambic, and abbey ales can all have this wild, funky yeast. Following are a few good examples of Belgian ales.

>> **Tank 7:** Boulevard Brewing Company was founded in 1989 in Kansas City, Missouri. After a vacation in Europe, founder John McDonald came home with a thirst for German and Belgian beers. The brewery grew steadily over the years, and in 2014 they merged with the legendary Moortgat Duvel, maker of the equally legendary Belgian beer. Tank 7 is an American saison. This is an American riff on the Belgian style. Very light in body, Tank 7 is fruity, slightly grassy, and has some pepper on the finish.

>> **La Fin du Monde:** Unibroue is a Canadian brewery based out of Chambly, Quebec. In 1993, their mission from the onset was to build a brewery that specialized in Belgian abbey-style beers. La Fin du Monde is their flagship beer and is one of the most awarded Canadian beers. This beer is mildly hoppy and medium-bodied, and it has flavors of spice, grass, fruit, and some alcohol.

>> **Chimay:** Chimay is a Trappist brewery located in Scourmont Abbey. The brewery was founded in 1862 and specializes in abbey-style Belgian ale. The Chimay Red is a dark brown dubbel. It has a strong flavor of dried fruit, apricot, brown sugar, spice, and some alcohol.

The spectrum of Belgian beers is very broad and diverse, but one thing that is common across the ales listed here is that they have spice notes that are similar due to the types of yeast used. They are all also elevated in alcohol, so proceed with caution.

TIP

Pair these beers with soft cheeses like Brie or Saint-André. You can also pair them with hard cheeses like pecorino or aged Parmesan, Swiss, and Gruyère. Try Belgian ales with prosciutto-wrapped figs.

India pale ale

Every craft beer lover at one point or another falls in love with the dank, floral, bitter flavor of over-hopped beers. India Pale Ale, or IPA, is a name that was given to beers that were brewed with extra grain to ferment to a higher alcohol level, and over-hopped so as to preserve them for the long journey from England to the British colonies in India. Today, these beers aren't being shipped in wooden casks in the belly of wooden ships. Instead, they are big beers with *huge* floral notes from hops. The fresher they are consumed, the better.

There are numerous types of IPA. The more current releases focus a lot more on hop profile. Single-hop IPA is a great way to showcase the different nuances of hops. American IPAs tend to be higher in calories (ugh), higher in alcohol (yay), and bitter. (But not bitter like 'skunked' bitter, bitter in a refreshing way.) IPA can bring forth many different flavors, depending on the hops. Some hops present fruit flavors, citrus, melon, or more herbal and medicinal qualities. Following are some great IPAs to try.

>> **Torpedo Extra IPA:** Founded in Chico, California, Sierra Nevada Brewing Company is a powerhouse of hoppy beers. To this day, they are one of the top-ten largest privately owned breweries in America. Sierra Nevada Torpedo is an extra IPA. It is a crisp, malty beer with medium-plus body. Possessing a very large, fragrant nose of pine, herbs, and citrus, it is a bitter beer with big floral flavors.

>> **60 Minute IPA:** Dogfish Head brewery was founded in 1995 in Milton, Delaware. Their beers are all very unusual in one way or another, and the 60 Minute IPA is no different. It is an American IPA that is continually hopped for the duration of the 60-minute boil. This means that as the wort is boiled, hops are continually added in small amounts for 60 minutes. This adds a ton of hop flavor, aroma, and some increased bitterness. There are also big pine and citrus flavors in this beer.

>> **Pliny the Elder:** Russian River Brewing Company was founded by Korbel Champagne in 1997 in the Russian River Valley of Sonoma County, California. In 2004 they decided to get out of the beer business and transferred the brewery to Vinnie Cilurzo and his wife Natalie. Pliny the Elder was one of the first commercially produced Double (Imperial) IPAs brewed in America, and it immediately won numerous awards. Today it is regarded as one of the best IPAs in the world. This is a dry beer with big citrus and pine flavors. Find it, drink it.

IPAs have big, intense flavors and aromas, and they pair really well with pizza with red sauce. Pair IPA with blue cheese, Parmesan, pecorino, and sharp cheddar. Salamis made with hops are not good, but hoppy beers with salamis are great. Spicy, cured meats are also a nice companion.

American stouts

If you like dark beer, the American stout is about as dark as it can get. In a beer lineup, it stands out like a sore thumb. American stout beers are thick, dark, and rich. They're ideal for the cold winters, not a hot beach. Some of the barley in American stouts is heavily roasted. This imparts not only color but also dark flavors into the beer; think chocolate, coffee, toffee, prune, and maybe soy sauce (sometimes).

American stouts have a good deal of hops to balance out the sweetness. Stouts are my favorite. I can drink them in the summertime in air-conditioning. They truly are hibernation beers. The alcohol levels tend to be quite elevated in stouts. The imperial stouts, which are essentially "double" versions of the beer, are often aged in bourbon barrels to impart vanilla and caramel flavors. They are also often finished with cocoa nibs to take that chocolate flavor to the next level.

If you're not familiar with American stouts, give these a try.

» **Breakfast Stout:** Founders Brewing Company was founded in 1997 in Grand Rapids, Michigan, by Mike Stevens and Dave Engbers. Like most upstart American breweries at that time, they started small and grew steadily. Their beers are some of my favorites, with the Breakfast Stout ranking as my number-one American stout. It is brewed with coffee and chocolate, which you taste in the glass.

» **Black Chocolate Stout:** The Brooklyn Brewery is located in Brooklyn, New York, and was founded in the late 1980s by Steve Hindy and Tom Potter. Their Black Chocolate Stout is a limited-release Russian Imperial Stout (RIS). The RIS was originally made with higher amounts of hops and alcohol to preserve it for travel. This beer has an amazing dark-chocolate aroma and flavor through the addition of several different types of toasted barley.

» **Kalamazoo Stout:** Bell's Brewery in Kalamazoo, Michigan, is a fantastic brewery responsible for numerous legendary beers, and Kalamazoo Stout is no exception. This is a great representation of the American stout style. It is full bodied and has aromas of dark chocolate and fresh coffee.

Stouts are big and bold beers with dark, toasted flavors of bitter chocolate, espresso, and sometimes spice, vanilla, and smoke. They can pair nicely with soft, creamy cheeses like Brie and Saint-André, or they can go incredibly well with blue cheeses. Pair them with smoked meats and see what happens!

Sours

Pucker up, buttercup. Sour beers have been around for quite some time, but in the last 15 years their popularity has grown at a fever pitch. Sour beers are exactly what they sound like: beers that are tart. The souring is caused by wild yeast strains (*Lactobacillus*, *Pediococcus*) that "infect" the beer and cause the souring. There are several traditional styles of sour ales that include Berliner Weisse, Gose, Flanders red ale, lambic, and American wild ales. Each type has its own unique tartness and characteristics.

These beers are often pampered much like wine is. Fruit can be added; in the case of lambic beers, cherry is added to make kriek, and raspberry to make framboise. Berliner Weisse is generally a low-alcohol beer that is mildly sour and often served with fruit syrups. Flanders ales are sour beers aged in oak barrels. Then there are the American sours. There are no real regulations or guidelines in the world of American wild ales, so the sky is the limit.

>> **Supplication:** Russian River Brewing Company is a world-class brewery responsible for making Pliny the Elder (see earlier). They are also world renowned for their sour beers. Supplication is a brown ale that is stored in Pinot Noir barrels from Sonoma County wineries, and it is aged for about a year with sour cherries and several funky yeast strains. What you get is a tart, fruity, delightful beer that is age-worthy like wine and also delicious young.

>> **Fou'Foune:** Probably the most legendary brewery among sour fans is Cantillon Brewery. They are located in the Belgian countryside, and their beers are widely sought after in the United States. The Fou'Foune is a lambic beer that is aged for 18 to 20 months, for a portion of that time with Bergeron apricots. This is a tart beer with gentle notes of spice and mild apricot. If you can find one, call some friends and share it.

>> **La Folie:** The New Belgium Brewing Company was founded in Fort Collins, Colorado. The brewery is world renowned for several of their Belgian-style ales, their flagship being the Fat Tire Amber Ale. La Folie is a sour, brown ale that ages slowly in large oak barrels for 1 to 3 years. In the glass, it is mahogany in color and has a big, tart nose and a palate of sour apple, cherry, and plum.

TIP

Pair sour beers with stinky cheese. Yes, stinky, aged, washed-rind cheeses, such as taleggio, aged Brie, and Limburger. Goat cheese is also great because it has a higher acid content. Sour beers will also go nicely with salty, cured meats. Try sours with some spicy salami as well.

4

The Part of Tens

Ten inexpensive wines guaranteed to impress your friends.

Ten fantastic meats that you must try.

Chapter **11**

Ten Wines Under $25 to Impress Your Guests

very year, over one million different wines are produced commercially. If you live in the United States, chances are good that less than five percent of those wines even make it into your state. But let's be honest: 50,000 different wines is a lot of variety to make your way through, and for this reason it can be a daunting task to find epic wines. There isn't necessarily a direct correlation between price and quality, but I will say that the concentration of delicious wines is far greater the further you go above $25 — that is, until you get to a price point where hype, exclusivity, and marketing take over.

So, in an ocean of grape juice, how do you find the wines with the killer quality-to-price ratio (QPR)? Well, you can just start buying wines and seeing what you like, but this can quickly get expensive. The other option is to rely on the opinions of others, but you know what they say about opinions: They are a lot like elbows; we all have them. Numerous wine reviewers have gained clout in the wine world over the years by drinking wines and pontificating about their qualities. Scoring systems have been adapted, and wine marketers have latched onto chasing the scores because they are a simple way to communicate the implied quality of a wine to the average person.

Our opinions are relative to our own personal preferences and biases. This has fueled the rise of numerous wine reviewers as people find that their palates and preferences align with one reviewer over another. Having said that, this chapter is intended to draw your attention to ten different wines that, at the publishing of this book, are under $25. These wines are, in my opinion, good values at their respective price points. They are ranked in no particular order, and I was paid no money to include them. I have, however, consumed a couple of swimming pools worth of wine for under $50 a bottle, and these bottles, when sampled, were well worth the sticker price.

Joseph Drouhin Saint-Véran Chardonnay

Maison Joseph Drouhin is a wine producer based in the region of Beaune in Burgundy, France. They started in 1880 and slowly grew over the years, acquiring parcels of land throughout Burgundy, and recently in the United States. Saint-Véran is a small, denoted wine-making area in the Mâconnais region of Burgundy. Burgundy is considered to be the home of Chardonnay and Pinot Noir, and these two grapes account for the bulk of all wine production in the Burgundy region.

Joseph Drouhin Saint-Véran Chardonnay is a delightfully refreshing Chardonnay that is aged in 100-percent stainless-steel vats, which plays a role in keeping this wine crisp and bright. The wine gives off fresh flowers and fruit on the nose, and pleasant fruit flavors like lemon, yellow apple, and melon on the palate. If you've ever said, "I don't like Chardonnay," try this wine and let it coax you back. If you love Chardonnay, this may qualify as a "patio pounder." Drink with fish, soft cheese, salty ham, and hard, mild salamis.

Pico Maccario Lavignone Barbera d'Asti

Brothers Pico and Vitaliano launched Pico Maccario in 1997 out of a desire to produce wine with their grapes rather than just selling them to other wine makers. Their wines are all Barbera and Barbera-based blends. Barbera is an Italian grape that has increased in notoriety, along with many of Italy's wines, over the past few decades. The grape has historically been used for making table wines in the Piedmont region of Italy that can be consumed young and in larger quantities at your local trattoria.

Barbera is now getting better treatment in the vineyard and in the winery as methods that were applied toward the king and queen of Piedmont grapes, Barolo and Barbaresco, are now being applied to other grapes like Barbera. Barbera is a vibrant, fruit-forward grape that really shines in the bottle with a little TLC, and the *Pico Maccario Lavignone Barbera d'Asti* is a great example of this. This wine is made from grapes that are grown in the Asti region of Piedmont, a wine-making region in the northwestern part of Italy.

The Lavignon Barbera d'Asti is a bright, aromatic wine that is medium bodied, with moderate tannin and moderate alcohol. The wine has a nose of fresh cherries and blue flowers. On the palate you will find those cherries again, along with slightly earthy characteristics that remind you of place. This is a versatile wine that goes great with salted meats, grilled fish, and pastas with red sauce or cream sauce. Or you can just drink it on an afternoon because the sun is shining.

Substance Cabernet

Substance Cabernet is a wine line from Charles Smith, a wine-making luminary from the state of Washington. He is a wine maker and brilliant businessman who started making wines in 1999 and released his first wine in 2001. Since then, Smith has gone on to grow what many view as an empire of vino in Washington state. His style of wine making is big and bold, and much of what he makes, even at a large scale, is of good to great quality. His Substance line is no exception.

Substance is 100-percent Cabernet Sauvignon from the Columbia Valley AVA (American Viticultural Area). The grapes are sourced from multiple vineyards in the area and are picked at the peak of ripeness. The Columbia Valley AVA is dry, with warm days and cooler nights, and they get piles of sunshine. Substance Cabernet is a big, bold wine. On the nose, you will find a cornucopia of smells like black cherry, coffee, baking spices, and pipe tobacco. On the palate, you will taste black cherry, blackberry, blueberry, earthy characteristics, spices, and licorice.

This is a full-bodied wine with a good amount of tannin and slightly elevated alcohol (14 percent). It is a killer wine, especially for the price, and it goes nicely with smoked meats, steak, and bold, hard cheeses.

Gouguenheim Malbec Reserva

The various wine regions in Argentina are so picturesque that they seem like something out of a storybook. The most well-known region in Argentina is located near Mendoza. This high-altitude region is a desert that is watered almost exclusively by the melt water from the Andes Mountains. The high-altitude climate, while cooler than at sea level, is extremely sunny, resulting in warm days and cool nights. Grapes can stay on the vine to full ripeness, and the temperature fluctuations allow them to maintain a good level of acid. All of these factors play a harmonious role in producing Malbec of superior quality.

In 2002, Patricio Gouguenheim jumped ship on his day-job to pursue his passion and become a wine grower and maker. Gouguenheim wines are grown and made in the Valle de Uco at an elevation of 3600 feet above sea level. *Gouguenheim Malbec Reserva* is a delightful red wine of 100-percent Malbec. The color is deep purple and gives off inviting aromas of cherry, blueberry, and earthy coffee notes. On the palate, you will find red cherry, black cherry, blueberry, blue flowers, and baking spices, which are imparted from six months of aging in new French-oak barrels. Even though this delightful juice hits peak ripeness on the vine, the wine itself is fermented to a modest 13- to 13.5-percent alcohol.

This wine benefits from some time swirling in the glass and will pair nicely with blue cheese, grilled burgers, herbed cheese, and cured meats.

Pierre Sparr Cremant Rosé

Pierre Sparr is a winery in the Alsace region of France that was started in 1680 by Jean Sparr, and since then has passed through nine generations of Sparr family wine makers until the 1900s, when it was taken over by Pierre Sparr. Pierre was a pioneer in the Alsace region who was committed to the family business and the craft of wine making. He saw his winery through the destruction of World War II, and with the help of his sons and family, he was able to replant, rebuild, and continue the legacy of the Sparr winery to the present day.

The Alsace region sits in the rain shadow of the Vosges Mountains, which lie to the west, while the Rhine River borders its eastern side. This region is very far north, and while it is dry, it does stay cool year-round. Ripening can be difficult, and the region is really best for white varietals like Riesling, Gewürztraminer, Pinot Gris, Pinot Blanc, and Sylvaner, but Pinot Noir can also grow here and actually accounts for nearly ten percent of total grape production.

Pierre Sparr Cremant Rosé is a sparkling wine made in the Champagne method with 100-percent Pinot Noir. The juice is allowed to sit on the grape skins to extract just enough color to give it a delightful salmon-pink hue. The wine is aged for about 18 months in the bottle on the lees (yeast), which provides the delightful bready characteristics. On both the nose and palate, you'll find subtle hints of strawberry, raspberry, almond, and bread. This wine is fresh, vibrant, and delicious, and it can be consumed with almost anything. I love this wine.

Theorize Zinfandel

If you love a good glass of wine and you've never been to Napa Valley, I would encourage you to visit. It's definitely worth the trip at least once in your life. This is a beautiful region of California and probably the most famous in the United States. This wine-growing region started capturing the attention of wine lovers around the globe after several Napa wines beat out French wines in a blind tasting in France. (Google "Judgement of Paris.")

Napa Valley is a large valley that is bordered by the Vaca Mountains to the east and the Mayacamas Mountains to the west. The valley closes off in the north and is open all the way south to San Pablo Bay. Fog and cloud cover roll into the valley from the south at night, and burn off in the late morning. This fog has a tempering effect on the hot, sunny days of summertime. Napa Valley gets very little water, so the vines have to work pretty hard to create quality fruit. This struggle is important to creating concentrated, flavorful juice.

Cabernet Sauvignon is the star of the show in Napa Valley, but the Zinfandel grape also does exceptionally well there. This grape, when cultivated correctly, produces full-bodied, dark, jammy wines, and *Theorize Zinfandel* is no exception. This delightful wine is the brainchild of Jean Hoefliger, the wine maker behind The Debate, a premier wine project from Alpha Omega Winery. Theorize is made with 100-percent California Zinfandel, with the bulk of the juice coming from Napa Valley. It is aged for ten months in 100-percent French oak, almost half of which is new oak.

On the nose, Theorize has bold aromas of ripe, dark cherries, prunes, black pepper, and pipe tobacco. On the palate there is a lot going on, with combinations of ripe, dark-red cherries and blackberries and lingering hints of vanilla and spice. This is a full-bodied wine, and the alcohol is slightly elevated, at 14.5 percent. Drink this wine with smoked meats, barbeque, ribs, brisket, and smoked sausage.

Roger Neveu Sancerre

Sancerre is a small wine region in the Loire Valley of France. If you were to fly a plane about 100 miles due south of Paris, you would hit it. Sancerre is just to the west of the Loire River and is well known for growing Sauvignon blanc. A lot of places in the world grow it, but I generally prefer Sauvignon blanc from Sancerre. Domain Roger Neveu is a great winery located in Sancerre. Although their history dates back to the 1600s, the modern incarnation of the estate dates back to 1977, when Roger brought Domain back to life.

The Sancerre region is known for great Sauvignon blanc because the cooler climate, limestone soil, and southern-facing hillsides create ideal conditions for growing the grapes for this crisp, refreshing wine. *Roger Neveu Sancerre* is a fantastic representation of the grape and place where it is grown. On the nose, you will immediately smell fresh lemon zest, peach skin, and white flowers. On the palate you will get some lemony acidity, lemon zest, ripe peaches, and minerals that almost tickle the tip of your tongue.

This is a killer wine, especially when it is hot outside. It goes great with briny oysters, lobster, crab, and other seafood. Drink it with salmon cooked with dill and lemon, and you might forget your name. Maybe.

Angelo Negro Angelin Langhe Nebbiolo

Langhe is a hilly area to the south and east of the Tanaro River in the Piedmont region of Italy. It is a beautiful area that is home to delicious cheeses, white truffles of Alba, and wine, of course! Nebbiolo is the grape of Piedmont and is used to make wine in the Barolo and Barbaresco regions. It is a small, black grape that packs a punch. This grape is believed to be at its best when raised within the Barolo or Barbaresco regions. In these areas, some of the world's most age-worthy wines are produced. However, the Nebbiolo that is being cultivated in the Langhe region of Piedmont is much more capable of being consumed a lot earlier.

The Negro family is one of several families that have been producing wine in the Langhe region for generations. Their family records date back to the 1670s, when the family was cultivating vineyards on the same land that housed the winery and 70 hectares of vineyard that the family still works today. That's an amazing familial legacy! Today they are making fantastic wines that can be consumed on release or aged for a few years.

Angelo Negro Angelin Langhe Nebbiolo also simply known as "Angelin," is 100-percent Nebbiolo grown on the estate. This is a delightful wine that is fresh and vibrant! On the nose you will find rose, a tell-tale sign of Nebbiolo, as well as blackberry, anise, and hints of tar. On the palate you'll find fresh fruits like cherry and tart blackberry, and some light, floral characteristics. This is a delightful wine that can be consumed with salty meats, salami with truffle, and pasta with sauce.

Mestres 1312 Cava Brut Reserva

Wine has been in production in Spain for quite some time. Archaeologists have uncovered evidence dating back to the 6th century that shows the cultivation of Chardonnay. Imagine that: wine making 1500 years ago in Spain! There are several amazing wine regions in Spain, and Penedes is the region of concern when it comes to Cava. Penedes is located in the Catalonia region, which is in the northwestern part of Spain, close to the border with France.

Cava is made with the indigenous grapes Xarel-lo, Parellada, and Macabeu. It is a sparkling wine made in a similar manner to Champagne. The Mestres family has an interesting story because they were the first wine producers to register the word "Cava." Records show that it was used by them in 1959 to inform consumers that this was a sparkling wine aged in a cellar, "Vins de Cava." The Mestres family produces their Cava largely by hand, and this great care surely translates to the bottle!

Mestres 1312 Reserva Brut ages for 20 months in the bottle on the lees (yeast) before release! This wine offers a tremendous bang for the buck! On the nose you get a bouquet of green apples, white flowers, stone fruit, and toast. On the palate the wine is bright, bubbly, and delicious. Flavors of toasted nuts, bread, apples, and citrus zest come through. You don't need a special occasion to drink sparkling wine; it pairs with almost everything, and it's refreshing and delicious. Just pop it. Drink this wine with fresh, spicy sausage, jamon, chorizo, preserved fish, fresh fish, and oysters.

Campuget 1753 Rosé

The Château de Campuget and winery are located in a small wine-making region called Costières de Nîmes in the Rhône Valley region of France. This small wine region used to be considered part of the Languedoc region of France, but the wines more closely resembled those of the Rhône Valley, so it was shifted to become part of the Rhône Valley. This area is warm and humid thanks to its proximity to the Mediterranean Sea. The soil is largely comprised of round pebbles, sand, and red shale. The heat and humidity are tempered in the vineyard by the ocean breezes that come inland.

Campuget 1753 Rosé is a blend of the red grape, Syrah, and the white grape, Vermentino. The heat, sun, and access to water that characterize this region make it easy to grow these grapes. The light-pink color comes from the short amount of time the juice has in contact with the skins of the Syrah grape. The true challenge is growing ripe fruit that maintains acidity so that the resulting wines aren't flabby and lacking character. The Campuget 1753 Rosé is definitely not that! This rosé is a warm-weather patio wine for sure!

Campuget should be consumed within one year of release. It is a fresh wine with nice aromas of citrus and subtle red fruit on the nose. On the palate the wine is fresh and crisp. You will find hints of red fruit, citrus, and a slight herbal quality. This wine goes great with salty cold cuts, grilled fish, and smoked fish.

Chapter **12**

Ten Meats You Must Try

I have been fortunate to be able to do a bit of traveling around the United States and around the world. I've been able to set foot on every continent with the exception of Antarctica. One of the things I love the most about traveling is visiting the local grocery stores. You can learn a lot about where you are just by seeing what the locals eat. Next time you travel, try that. It doesn't matter if it is to another state, or to another country; just take a peek at what is in the nearest grocery store and see what you can see.

This chapter doesn't offer a comprehensive list of the greatest meats in the world. It just contains a list of meats that I think are really good and should be tried at some point. Many of the foods are tied to a special memory, but I didn't list them simply because of nostalgia. Everything in this list is delicious, and if you are able to, you should track some of them down to try for yourself. Keep in mind that this list is in no particular order.

La Quercia Acorn Edition Prosciutto

Iowa has a meat-producing gem that may sneak under the radar for many people. The company is called La Quercia. The word itself is Italian for "The Oak," and the inspiration for the name came from the time that founders Herb and Kathy Eckhouse spent living in Italy. During their time abroad, they got to see the love and care that went into the production of Prosciutto di Parma, and how that attention to detail could produce something as delicious and sublime as that famed Italian ham. When they came back to the U.S., they wanted to start La Quercia to focus on making American hams in the tradition of Parma.

La Quercia is a cool company for a few reasons: They've spent a lot of time focusing on environmental sustainability. They also work with farmers in Iowa that raise their pigs to a very particular specification. This is to ensure that the ingredients they use to make their award-winning hams are of the utmost quality. It is also to ensure that they are supporting farmers that incorporate sustainability into their practices!

Eating the Acorn Edition Prosciutto (shown in Figure 12-1) is a mind-boggling experience. These hams come from a Tamworth pig, which is a heritage breed pig. These pigs are pasture-raised on a farm. What makes them truly special is that they spend time foraging an Ozark Mountain hillside, where acorns and hickory nuts make up an estimated 65 to 70 percent of their diet. This nutty diet imparts a very nutty characteristic into the flavor of these hams. Once they are dispatched, the hams are salted and slowly dried over 30 to 36 months. The long drying time allows for some very complex and delicious flavors to develop in the flesh of this legendary ham. If you can find some, try it!

FIGURE 12-1: La Quercia acorn-fed prosciutto.

Mark LaFay

Smoking Goose Delaware Fireball

Over ten years ago, Chris Eley and his wife, Mollie, opened up a craft butcher shop in Indianapolis, Indiana. They provided pasture-raised proteins, epic sandwiches, miscellaneous gourmet ingredients and products, and a carefully curated selection of beers and wines. From this space, Chris started producing several types of dry-cured, whole-muscle meats as well as dry-cured, fermented sausages. The success of their products grew to the point where they launched a USDA-inspected, wholesale charcuterie company called Smoking Goose.

In those early days, many of the products made at Goose the Market were only available on a limited basis because of the space they needed to keep up with growing demand. That meant that if you found something you loved, you needed to buy it on release. That, for me, was the Delaware Fireball (Figure 12-2). The Delaware Fireball is a pork salami formed in the shape of a ball and wrapped in caul fat. Essentially, it is a "crepinette" of salami. The salami is seasoned with chilis and hot pepper powders, cold smoked, and then fermented and dried. The Delaware Fireball is a delightful salami with enough spice to warm you up but not blow you out.

FIGURE 12-2: Smoking Goose Delaware Fireball.

Corrie E. Cook for Goose the Market and Smoking Goose

Mousse de Foie Gras de Canard

Years ago, my wife and I made a quick weekend getaway to Montreal. It was sort of a whirlwind trip because we got stranded in Chicago overnight due to a flight cancellation. When we got to Montreal, we proceeded to cover as much ground as possible. I've always enjoyed visiting the central markets located in many of Canada's large cities. We stopped by the Atwater Market, which is located down by the river and near the old town of Montreal. In the upstairs, there is a small shop that specializes in terrines and pâtés. The shop was something to see, and I wish I had taken more photos when we were there (Figure 12-3 gives you a general idea of their variety of products).

I'm a big fan of foie gras. It's a somewhat controversial product because of how it is produced. If you are unfamiliar, here's the gist: Foie gras is the liver of a goose or duck that is extremely fatty. The liver gets this way by over-feeding the birds. When the birds are dispatched, the liver is saved and there you have it: foie gras. The flavor is out of control: rich, fatty, savory, and velvety. The liver flavor is very, very mild.

FIGURE 12-3:
Terrine and Pâtés shop in Montreal.

Mark LaFay

This shop makes a *mousse de foie gras de canard*. A mousse is a pâté that is finely puréed and strained so that the texture is extremely smooth and creamy. This particular mousse is made with duck foie gras. The resulting pâté is subtle, rich, and out-of-control good. It goes great on crackers or toast. You can also top it with a savory flavor like cornichon or mustard, or you could go sweet and top it with fig jam. If you are ever in the area, this is worth a visit and a taste. However, you'll have to do a little searching for it.

Grammy Mae's Summer Sausage

When I was 14 years old, my father took me grouse hunting in Canada. We stayed at a little place called the Normandy Lodge just north of Wawa, Ontario. Take a look on the map; it is a pretty isolated area! On the way up, we stopped at a place in Wawa called Young's General Store. This store is probably what you are imagining it would be: a grocery, hardware store, knick-knack shop, and bait shop, offering something to anyone in the area or who is passing through. Young's was built in 1971 and has been a staple of the area ever since.

When we popped into the shop for some supplies before finishing our journey north, my father noticed that they had a pile of hard summer sausages in canvas bags. This pile was strategically placed in the middle of the store, and I'm pretty sure it was the sole source of the smoke fragrance that filled the shop. These were fermented summer sausages that had been dried hard and smoked aggressively. Handling these canvas-wrapped meat treats would make your hands smell of smoked meat for what seemed like days.

I wasn't a big salami fan as a kid, but holy cow, these were amazing, utterly amazing. They were tangy, salty, and smoky, and I've thought about them ever since. My father has been back a couple of times, but Grammy Mae's sausage (Figure 12-4) has never made the journey home to me; it has always been eaten en route. However, my good friend Tim Funston, upon my direction, paid a visit to the shop and loaded up. He's now a believer. If you are ever in Canada and you can get your hands on a hank or two of Grammy Mae's summer sausage, get two.

FIGURE 12-4:
Grammy Mae's
summer sausage.

Figatelli from Les Cochons Tout Ronds

On a trip to Montreal, my wife and I did some serious food tourism over a 48-hour period. We managed to eat our way through several restaurants, coffee shops, the legendary bagel bakery, and two of the general markets. While we were at the Marché Jean-Talon, we paid a visit to Les Cochons tout ronds, the creative outlet of chef Patrick Mathey. As you can see in Figure 12-5, they had an incredible selection of all sorts of sausages, both fresh and dry-cured, and whole-muscle charcuterie. It was piled high in the cases, and even though our knowledge of the French language was minimal, they were very willing to allow us to sample several different products — and they were all great.

We ended up purchasing numerous items to take back to our flat to munch on throughout the duration of our trip. One item, however, that blew me away was the figatelli. If you Google this sausage, you will find two different spellings and some slight variations, depending on the region where it is made, but at its roots, this is a Corsican sausage made with liver, pork, garlic, and spices. It can be made as a fresh sausage or a dry-cured sausage. What we got from Les Cochons tout ronds was the dry-cured version, and it was made from pork meat, liver, and heart. I don't believe they used pork blood, but I could have missed something in the translation at the time.

Mark LaFay

The salami is dark in color, and when you slice it open, you get a beautiful cross-section of the various bits and pieces that make the salami what it is. The flavor is rich, earthy, and herbaceous. We took home about 4 or 5 different salamis, but this one I couldn't stop eating. I don't know what it was, but after the flavor dissipated in my mouth, I was craving another bite. Patrick Mathey has a gift waiting for you in Montreal!

18-Month Prosciutto di Parma with Black Truffles

Italy is a magical place, especially if you are in search of incredible meats both fresh and dried. A few years back, my wife and I met up with some friends who were over in Italy for two months on a sabbatical. We managed to tag along for a week when they were staying in the former summer estate of the Medici family. This palatial estate had been split up into multiple units and housed a small culinary school for travellers who wanted to learn authentic methods and techniques. We used this place as a jumping-off point for our explorations throughout Tuscany.

In the middle of Florence near the Duomo is the central market. Inside the market are several different vendors. You can find olives, oils, wines, cutlery, fresh and cured meats, fresh produce, fish, bread, and so on. It almost feels like you've stepped back in time when you set foot inside. In the southeast corner of the market, there is a stall that specializes in cured hams — all sorts of cured hams, every Italian ham you could imagine. It's hard to explain how vast the selection is, but they have several different regional hams, and plenty of Parma ham aged for 18, 20, 24, 30 months, you name it!

What caught my eye was the 18-month ham with truffles. There are few things in life where I lack total self-control; one of those things is truffles. If you've never had truffles, I won't try to explain them to you. A truffle is a fungus that grows underground, often on the roots of different types of hardwoods trees. In Italy, truffles often grow on the roots of oak trees, and they have to be sniffed out by dogs or pigs in order to be found. They are earthy, musty, and funky, and you either love them or you hate them. I love them; oh, do I love them! This particular ham had every crack and crevice filled with minced black truffles. Each paper-thin slice wreaked of truffles and aged, salted Parma ham. If you love truffles, find this. If you aren't sure about truffles, find this. If you hate truffles, I feel bad for you.

Cinco Jotas Acorn-Fed Ibérico Ham

Italy is not the only country known for their hams. In Spain, ham is a way of life. There are numerous types of ham, and methods of production are enshrined in law. To put this in perspective, there are over 2000 producers of Serrano ham, a particular type of Spanish ham. Ibérico ham is a special type of ham that is made from the Ibérico pig. There are several tiers of quality associated with Ibérico ham that have to do with what the pigs are fed, how they are raised, and how long the hams are aged.

The top of the top, the crème de la crème, of Ibérico ham is the Ibérico de Bellota. This type of ham comes from Ibérico pigs that freely roam the oak forests along the border of Spain and Portugal, eating only acorns. The hams are then preserved and dried for at least three years before being released. The Ibérico Bellota is then further graded, based on whether or not the pigs are purebred Ibérico or if they are crossed with another breed.

Due to the USDA regulations regarding the importation of meats, Spanish ham was not easily found in the U.S. until around 2007. However, of the hams that are available, the Cinco Jotas (5Js) brand (Figure 12-6) is amazing. It is found in high-end restaurants, boutique gourmet Spanish groceries, and you can direct-order it. The last time I had 5J Ibérico ham, it was going for over $145 a pound. The flavor is out-of-control good, and if you can find it, try it!

FIGURE 12-6:
Cinco Jotas
Jamon.

Benton's Hickory Smoked Bacon

I would imagine that if there was pork royalty in the United States, the Bentons would be part of the family. Benton's Smoky Mountain Country Hams was started in 1947 by the late Albert H. Hicks. He was a dairy farmer who got into the business of curing and selling hams. Over time, his business expanded to produce a small array of products that included his famed Hickory Smoked Country Bacon.

There are a few different ways to make bacon. If you need a refresher on this, you might want to check Chapter 4 and read up on bacons. For the most part, the bacon that is widely available in the U.S. is cured and hot smoked. It is sold as potentially hazardous food that needs to be refrigerated until it is cooked. Benton's Hickory Smoked Country Bacon is very different. The process used to make their bacons is similar to how their country hams are made. First, they season the bellies with a blend of salt, sugar, and black pepper. The bellies are then hung in refrigeration for three weeks to dry out. After that, they are cold-smoked for two to three days with nothing but heavy hickory smoke. The bacon is then sliced, packed, and shipped.

It's a dry-cured bacon, which means that it contains much less water than traditional bacon. It is also not fully or even partially cooked during its production. The resulting product is rich in flavor, smoky, and out-of-this-world good. If you want to redefine bacon, start with Benton's. Thankfully, they ship.

Brooklyn Cured Bresaola

Brooklyn Cured is a butcher based in, you guessed it, Brooklyn, New York. They make small-batch sausages, smoked meat, and charcuterie, and they are darn good at it. Brooklyn Cured was started in 2010 by Scott Bridi, who worked in the restaurant industry in New York. One of the more notable places Scott called home for a time was the Gramercy Tavern, a renowned place known for meat craft and an epic rotating menu of delicious bites.

Brooklyn Cured makes an assortment of products that are intended to reflect the diversity of cultures found in their Brooklyn neighborhood. I first discovered Brooklyn Cured when I was catering an in-home wine dinner a few years ago. I wanted to bring in several new products, and I came across Brooklyn Cured. Until then, I hadn't found a bresaola that I could use on a charcuterie board. If you aren't familiar with bresaola, it's salted and air-dried beef, more often than not made from beef round or loin. Chapter 4 offers detailed instructions on how to make your own bresaola!

I love bresaola. It may be because I grew up on an inferior, air-dried beef product: chipped beef. Creamed chipped beef on toast was a common dinner in our home. My grandfather was in the navy in the Pacific during World War II, and I would imagine this was a common meal when he was home because it was a favorite of my dad's. But enough about chipped beef. Bresaola is not that. It's far more flavorful, and the Brooklyn Cured bresaola (shown in Figure 12-7) is a favorite of mine. It's dusted with dried porcini mushrooms, which gives it an earthiness that is righteous! If you're in Brooklyn, pick some up, or order it online!

Mole Salami

If you ever make it to Seattle, you need to pay a visit to Salumi. It's a salumeria and restaurant in the Pioneer Square neighborhood of downtown Seattle. The restaurant was founded by Armandino Batali, the father of Mario Batali. Needless to say, the place is amazing, and it garnered a lot of attention very quickly because of the names behind it. It was featured on *Anthony Bourdain: No Reservations* and also on the Travel Channel's *Adam Richman's Best Sandwich in America*. I had the pleasure of visiting the deli in January of 2019. I tried several of their salamis and also took several with me.

The one salami that really rocked my world was the Molé Salami (Figure 12-8). This salami is very unique and out-of-control good. It is seasoned with cocoa, cinnamon, and chili peppers. They started by making Molé Salami in-house, but the popularity of this salami and several other cured meats attracted some outside investment to fund expansion into a production facility and the formal launch of their new brand, CORO. If you ever make it to Seattle, you need to pay a visit to the Salumi Deli and give it a try. The Molé Salami alone is worth the visit!

FIGURE 12-8:
Salumi Molé
Salami.

Salumi

Index

Numbers

5Js (Cinco Jotas) brand, 205
18-Month Prosciutto di Parma with Black Truffles, 203–204
60 Minute IPA, 183

A

accouterments, 148–150
acidification, 33, 113–114
acids, 114–115
Acorn Edition Prosciutto, 197–198
add-on equipment, 10
air bubbles, 98
Alsace region, 192
American beer, 180–181, 184
American butchers, 45
American wine, 168–170, 173, 175
ancient salt mines, 48
andouille recipe, 107
Angelin, 194
Angelo Negro Angelin Langhe Nebbiolo, 194
Appendix A (FSIS), 30–31
appetizers, size of, 151
aroma, wine, 167
arrangements, for charcuterie board, 153–154
artisanal butcher shops, 44, 140–141
attachments, 10–11
auger, 8
Australia, Syrah wine, 171

B

back slopping, 114
bacon. *See also* pork
  Benton's Hickory Smoked, 205–206
  fresh-cured, 56–64
  Jowl Bacon recipe, 61–62
  Maple Bacon recipe, 59–60
  slicing in meat slicer, 15
  Smoked Belly Bacon recipe, 57–58
  Smoked Rasher Bacon recipe, 63–64
bacteria. *See also* pathogens
  controlling and killing, 30–31
  limited growth of, 19–20
  on salami, 113–114
Bactoferm F-RM-52 starter culture, 115–116
Bactoferm Mold-600, 123
Barbera wine, 190–191
basic salami recipe, 125–126
Batali, Armandino, 207
beef bung casing, 89
beef middles casing, 88
beer, 177–185
  American stouts, 184
  Belgian ales, 182–183
  India Pale Ale, 183–184
  making, 178–179
  pairing with food, 184
  Sours, 185
  standard American beer, 180–181
  wheat beer, 181–182
Beer Judge Certification Program, 179
Belgian ales, 182–183
Bell, Larry, 181
Bell's Brewery, 181, 184
Benton's Hickory Smoked Bacon, 205–206
Big box specialty grocery, 141
Bismarck, Otto von, 81
Black Chocolate Stout, 184
bleach-and-water mixture disinfectant, 21
blooming sausages, 100
Blue Moon beer, 181
Blue Stilton cheese, 144
body and hopper, 8

botulism, 33, 49

boudin blanc recipe, 109–110

Boulevard Brewing Company, 182

bowl chopper, 87

bratwurst, 103

Brazilian beef, 44

bread, 150

breakfast sausage, 102

Breakfast Stout, 184

bresaola, 75–76, 206–207

Bridi, Scott, 206

brie, 143

Broad Ripple Winter Market, 42

The Brooklyn Brewery, 184

Brooklyn Cured, 206–207

bubble knot, 121–122

buffalo chopper, 87

buffets, size of, 151

butcher shops, 44–45, 140–141

butcher supply stores, 22–23

Butcher-packer.com, 23

C

C. botulinum toxin, 34

Cabernet Sauvignon, 168–169

Calabrian chiles, 47

Campuget 1753 Rosé, 195–196

campylobacter, 33

Cantillon Brewery, 185

Carmel Winter Farmers Market, 42

casings, 88–93

  beef bung, 89

  beef middles, 88

  caring and prepping, 92–93

  cellulose, 89

  collagen, 90

  fibrous, 89, 90

  hog, 88

  natural, 88

  pre-tubed, 91

  sheep, 88

  where to buy, 90–92

Castelvetrano, 149

Cava, 195

Cave-aged Gouda cheese, 147

celery juice powder, 51

cellulose casing, 89

Centers for Disease Control and Prevention (CDC), 25

Central Restaurant Products, 23

Champagne Velvet beer, 180–181

charcuterie board, 139–159

  cheese options for, 142–147

  condiments and accouterments for, 148–150

  meat options for, 140–142

  putting together, 151

Chardonnay, 173–174

cheese, 142–147, 185

Chimay, 182

Cilurzo, Vinnie and Natalie, 183

Cinco Jotas (5Js) brand, 205

Cinco Jotas Acorn-Fed Ibérico Ham, 204–205

Claus' German Sausage and Meats, 44

cleaning

  bleach-and-water mixture disinfectant, 21

  hand washing, 25, 26

  hygiene for hazardous food, 26–28

  meat grinders, 20–22, 82

  prep-list, 29

  sanitation while stuffing sausage, 93

  work area, 28–29

Clostridium botulinum, 34

collagen casing, 90

collar, 45

Columbia Valley AVA, 191

commodity proteins, 40–41

community-supported agriculture (CSA) program, 41

condiments, 148–150

Coors Banquet, 180

coppa, 45, 73–74

CSA (community-supported agriculture) program, 41

G

gamey meat, 46–47

gas-burning smokers, 17

gear, 7–24

  cleaning, 29

  curing chambers, 17–19

  meat grinders, 8–13, 21

  meat slicer, 14–15

  sausage stuffers, 13–14

  scientific meters, 19–20

  shopping for locally, 22–23

  small wares, 20

  smokers, 16–17

  stuffers care, 21–22

German Riesling, 174

Goose the Market, 140–141

Gouda cheese, 145, 147

Gouguenheim, Patricio, 192

Gouguenheim Malbec Reserva wine, 191–192

gourmet grocery, 140–141

grains, in beer, 179

Gramercy Tavern, 206

Grammy Mae's Summer Sausage, 201–202

gravlax, 78–79

grinder hopper, 84, 85–86

grinders. *See* meat grinders

grist, 178

Gruyère cheese, 146

Guanciale recipe, 71–72

Gunthorp, Greg, 42

Gunthorp farms, 43

H

hard cheese, 146–147

hard salami, 113

hazardous food, 25–37

  controlling and killing bacteria, 30–31

  finding help with, 35–37

  before handling, 28–30

  pathogens, 33–35

  personal hygiene, 26–28

  protecting against pathogens, 30–33

  temperature control, 32–33

heritage animal breeds, 44–45

heritage protein, 39

Hickory Smoked Country Hams, 205–206

Hicks, Albert H., 205

Hindy, Steve, 184

hog casing, 88

hog farmers, 43

home oven, fermenting sausage in, 117

homemade curing chamber, 19

hopper, 84, 85–86

hops, 179

horns, 13

hot dog recipe, 111–112

hot smoking, 16

humidity and temperature control sensors, 19

hunting, 46

hygiene. *See* cleaning

I

Ibérico ham, 204

immersion circulator, 117

India Pale Ale, 183–184

ingredient, quality of, 39–51

IPAs, 183

Island Chicken Sausage recipe, 105

Italian butchers, 45

Italian Pinot Grigio wine, 176

J

Joseph Drouhin Saint-Véran Chardonnay, 190

Jowl Bacon recipe, 61–62

K

Kalamazoo Stout, 184

KitchenAid mixer attachment grinder, 9–11

knives, 8, 20

knots, for dry-cured meats, 67–68

kosher salt, 84

pH
  in fermented sausage, 114
  meters, 20, 118–121
  test strips, 118–120
picante recipe, 129–130
Pickled Shallot recipe, 156
pickles, 149, 155
Pico Maccario Lavignone Barbera d'Asti, 190–191
Pierre Sparr Cremant Rosé, 192
pink salt #1 and #2, 50
Pinot Grigio and Pinot Gris, 176
Pinot Noir, 169
pistons, 13
plate, on meat grinders, 8, 12
platters, for charcuterie board, 152–153
Pliny the Elder, 183
pork. *See also* bacon; sausages
  andouille recipe, 107
  boudin blanc recipe, 109–110
  bratwurst, 103
  breakfast sausage recipe, 102
  Cinco Jotas Acorn-Fed Ibérico Ham, 204–205
  coppa, 45, 73–74
  Figatelli, 202–203
  Guanciale recipe, 71–72
  Hickory Smoked Country Hams, 205–206
  Pancetta Tesa recipe, 69–70
  smoked pork sausage recipe, 108
Potter, Tom, 184
preserving, dry-cured meats, 66–67
pre-tubed casing, 91
Prima Pils, 180
prosciutto
  18-Month Prosciutto di Parma with Black
    Truffles, 203–204
  La Quercia Acorn Edition Prosciutto, 197–198
proteins, 49. See also types of proteins
  for charcuterie board, 140–142
  commodity proteins, 40–41
  controlling and killing bacteria on, 30
  heritage protein, 39
  pasture-raised proteins, 46–47

purchasing from butcher shop, 44–45
  purchasing from farmers, 41–44
  wild game, 46–47
protein-to-fat ratio, 82

Q

quality-to-price ratio (QPR), 189
quick kill, 46–47
Quick Pickle Chips recipe, 155

R

ready-made dry-curing chamber, 18
red wine, 166–171
  Cabernet Sauvignon, 168–169
  Merlot, 169–170
  Pinot Noir, 169
  Sangiovese, 171
  Syrah, 170–171
regenerative farming, 43
rendering, 83
Riesling, 174–175
Roger Neveu Sancerre, 193–194
Romano cheese, 147
Rosemary Toasted Marcona Almonds recipe, 159
rubber gasket, 22
Russian River Brewing Company, 183, 185

S

Saint-André cheese, 143
salami, 113–136. *See also* sausages
  basic salami recipe, 125–126
  Delaware Fireball, 199
  drying, 124
  fermenting, 114–121
  Finocchiona recipe, 127–128
  good mold on, 122–123
  Grammy Mae's Summer Sausage, 201–202
  with IPAs, 184
  lowering pH, 20
  Milano-style salami recipe, 135–136

About the Author

Mark LaFay has entrepreneurialism running through his veins. From grade school to now, LaFay has created and run small businesses that have taken him and his products around the world. LaFay built businesses in the music industry, producing hundreds of events in Central Indiana and developing numerous musical acts into internationally touring and recognized groups. LaFay was co-founder of Lectio (http://mylectio.com), a software startup and mobile application built to encourage independent reading for students with language-related learning disabilities; and he was a co-founder of Roust, a social network for people interested in discussing politics, policy, religion, and social issues. LaFay is the founder and owner of Old Major Market, an Indianapolis-based virtual butcher shop specializing in sausage, bacon, cured meats, and artisanal provisions. LaFay is also a Certified Sommelier in the Court of Master Sommeliers.

Dedication

I dedicate this book to my beautiful, loving wife, Carrie LaFay; my sons, Harvey Clayton LaFay and Benjamin Robert LaFay; as well as my in-utero daughter (we still don't have a name for you, but I'm sure you'll be awesome).

Author's Acknowledgments

In 2016 I got the crazy idea to start a business that would lead to a slower pace of life. I wanted it to be the convergence of all the things that I was passionate about: meat craft, wine, foraging, artisanal foods, and the like. I wanted to support local farmers that were ethically raising their critters. I wanted to connect people to good food. At the time, I had no idea what that would look like or how we would get there, but I had a vision, encouragement from my wife, support from mentors, and so off we went. We began the task of building Old Major Market out of nothing, and we started with one product: bacon.

We are in our fifth year now. We are working hard and having a great time. We are a USDA-inspected producer of sausages and bacon, and we have a whole slew of retail ready-to-eat products. The journey so far has been one continual learning process, and we are excited to see where the future will take us. But we couldn't have gotten here if it weren't for a whole long list of folks. To my wife Carrie: You are the love of my life, and I couldn't do any of this without your love and support. Thank you for encouraging me to pursue my passions and for being willing to ride the entrepreneurial roller coaster with me. My right-hand man, Cody Jefferson, you make it happen week after week. I wouldn't want to do this without you. Chris Eley, thank you for your friendship and willingness to let me pick your brain and learn from your experiences. Greg Gunthorp, you are a master of HACCP, an incredible resource, a champion for the small family farmer, and most importantly a great encourager. Dr. Bough and the team at INBOAH, y'all are doing good work that is often thankless. Thank you for always going above and beyond. Bill Oesterle, thank you for giving us a place where we could grow and for making us stick to the lean methodology. Paul Thrift, I know you think I'm crazy, but hey, you're eating and drinking better these days. Thank you for your friendship, support, and advocacy. Kelly Hendricks, you're a great friend and mentor.

This is starting to feel like the "thank you section" in the liner notes of a CD — oh well. There are so many people to acknowledge: Jenn & Sully, Echo, Robyn Bognar, Robbie Davis (you bad man, you), Mike Strader, Chiko The Man, Don, Jamie Ridpath, Katharyn, Kara, go #TeamMeat! Carmel, Broad Ripple, Fishers, and Zionsville Farmers Market staff, Shane and everyone at Piazza (especially my brother in law, John Nuyen), Blair and everyone at Delco. Nason Frizell at Central Restaurant Products. Travis Hartley, you are a good man. Everyone at FWE, y'all make great gear, but your smokers are our favorite. Nick Carter and the team at Marketwagon. BBQ Team Old Major Market: Jeff Krajewski, Tim Funston, Brady Smith. Tim Dooley, Josh Stoneking, Tyler Herald, Kristian Andersen, Mike Fitzgerald, The Indianapolis Opera, Yeti Coolers, GMC Trucks, Sausagemaker.com, and every customer, from the bottom of my heart, thank you.

Publisher's Acknowledgments

Acquisitions Editor: Katie Mohr

Editorial Project Manager and Development Editor: Christina N. Guthrie

Copy Editor: Marylouise Wiack

Production Editor: Siddique Shaik

Photographer: David Pluimer

Cover Photos: © Dave Pluimer

Take dummies with you everywhere you go!

Whether you are excited about e-books, want more from the web, must have your mobile apps, or are swept up in social media, dummies makes everything easier.

Find us online!

dummies.com

Leverage the power

Dummies is the global leader in the reference category and one of the most trusted and highly regarded brands in the world. No longer just focused on books, customers now have access to the dummies content they need in the format they want. Together we'll craft a solution that engages your customers, stands out from the competition, and helps you meet your goals.

Advertising & Sponsorships

Connect with an engaged audience on a powerful multimedia site, and position your message alongside expert how-to content. Dummies.com is a one-stop shop for free, online information and know-how curated by a team of experts.

- Targeted ads
- Video
- Email Marketing
- Microsites
- Sweepstakes sponsorship

20 MILLION PAGE VIEWS EVERY SINGLE MONTH

15 MILLION UNIQUE VISITORS PER MONTH

43% OF ALL VISITORS ACCESS THE SITE VIA THEIR MOBILE DEVICES

700,000 NEWSLETTER SUBSCRIPTIONS TO THE INBOXES OF

300,000 UNIQUE INDIVIDUALS EVERY WEEK

PERSONAL ENRICHMENT

Staying Sharp
9781119187790
USA $26.00
CAN $31.99
UK £19.99

Facebook
9781119179030
USA $21.99
CAN $25.99
UK £16.99

Guitar
9781119293354
USA $24.99
CAN $29.99
UK £17.99

Investing
9781119293347
USA $22.99
CAN $27.99
UK £16.99

Beekeeping
9781119310068
USA $22.99
CAN $27.99
UK £16.99

Digital Photography
9781119235606
USA $24.99
CAN $29.99
UK £17.99

Meditation
9781119251163
USA $24.99
CAN $29.99
UK £17.99

Pregnancy
9781119235491
USA $26.99
CAN $31.99
UK £19.99

Samsung Galaxy S7
9781119279952
USA $24.99
CAN $29.99
UK £17.99

iPhone
9781119283133
USA $24.99
CAN $29.99
UK £17.99

Crocheting
9781119287117
USA $24.99
CAN $29.99
UK £16.99

Nutrition
9781119130246
USA $22.99
CAN $27.99
UK £16.99

PROFESSIONAL DEVELOPMENT

Windows 10
9781119311041
USA $24.99
CAN $29.99
UK £17.99

AutoCAD
9781119255796
USA $39.99
CAN $47.99
UK £27.99

Excel 2016
9781119293439
USA $26.99
CAN $31.99
UK £19.99

QuickBooks 2017
9781119281467
USA $26.99
CAN $31.99
UK £19.99

macOS Sierra
9781119280651
USA $29.99
CAN $35.99
UK £21.99

LinkedIn
9781119251132
USA $24.99
CAN $29.99
UK £17.99

Windows 10
9781119310563
USA $34.00
CAN $41.99
UK £24.99

SharePoint 2016
9781119181705
USA $29.99
CAN $35.99
UK £21.99

Fundamental Analysis
9781119263593
USA $26.99
CAN $31.99
UK £19.99

Networking
9781119257769
USA $29.99
CAN $35.99
UK £21.99

Office 2016
9781119293477
USA $26.99
CAN $31.99
UK £19.99

Office 365
9781119265313
USA $24.99
CAN $29.99
UK £17.99

Salesforce.com
9781119239314
USA $29.99
CAN $35.99
UK £21.99

Coding
9781119293323
USA $29.99
CAN $35.99
UK £21.99

dummies.com

dummies
A Wiley Brand

Learning Made Easy

ACADEMIC

9781119293576
USA $19.99
CAN $23.99
UK £15.99

9781119293637
USA $19.99
CAN $23.99
UK £15.99

9781119293491
USA $19.99
CAN $23.99
UK £15.99

9781119293460
USA $19.99
CAN $23.99
UK £15.99

9781119293590
USA $19.99
CAN $23.99
UK £15.99

9781119215844
USA $26.99
CAN $31.99
UK £19.99

9781119293378
USA $22.99
CAN $27.99
UK £16.99

9781119293521
USA $19.99
CAN $23.99
UK £15.99

9781119239178
USA $18.99
CAN $22.99
UK £14.99

9781119263883
USA $26.99
CAN $31.99
UK £19.99

Available Everywhere Books Are Sold

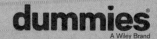